Child Psychology: A Very Short Introduction

VERY SHORT INTRODUCTIONS are for anyone wanting a stimulating and accessible way in to a new subject. They are written by experts, and have been translated into more than 40 different languages.

The Series began in 1995, and now covers a wide variety of topics in every discipline. The VSI library now contains over 350 volumes—a Very Short Introduction to everything from Psychology and Philosophy of Science to American History and Relativity—and continues to grow in every subject area.

Very Short Introductions available now:

Available soon:

For more information visit our website

www.oup.com/vsi/

Usha Goswami

CHILD PSYCHOLOGY

A Very Short Introduction

OXFORD
UNIVERSITY PRESS

OXFORD

UNIVERSITY PRESS

Great Clarendon Street, Oxford, OX2 6DP,
United Kingdom

Oxford University Press is a department of the University of Oxford.
It furthers the University's objective of excellence in research, scholarship,
and education by publishing worldwide. Oxford is a registered trade mark of
Oxford University Press in the UK and in certain other countries

First edition published in 2014

Impression: 1

Published in the United States of America by Oxford University Press
198 Madison Avenue, New York, NY 10016, United States of America

British Library Cataloguing in Publication Data

Data available

Library of Congress Control Number: 2014943270

ISBN 978-0-19-964659-3

Printed in Great Britain by
Ashford Colour Press Ltd, Gosport, Hampshire

To My Nephew
Zachary Thomas Goswami-Myerscough
In Memoriam

Contents

List of illustrations

The publisher and author apologize for any errors or omissions in this list. If contacted they will be happy to rectify these at the earliest opportunity.

Introduction

These are exciting times in child psychology. New techniques in brain imaging and genetics have given us important new insights into how children develop, think, and learn. This *Very Short Introduction* will summarize recent research on cognitive development and social/emotional development, focusing largely on the years 0–10. Cognitive development covers how children think, learn, and reason. Social/emotional development covers how children develop relationships, a sense of self, and the ability to control their emotions. Social and emotional well-being are intrinsically connected to cognitive growth. A child who is happy and secure in their family, peer group, and larger social environment is well placed to fulfil their cognitive potential. Children who are growing up in environments that make them anxious or fearful will find it more difficult to thrive, cognitively as well as emotionally.

Fortunately, creating optimal environments for young children requires factors that are available to everyone. These factors are time, patience, and love. Studies in child psychology have shown that *warmth* and *responsive contingency* are the key to optimal developmental outcomes. 'Responsive contingency' simply means responding to the overtures of the child immediately, and keeping the focus on the child's chosen focus of interest. Effective learning happens when the child experiences a 'supportive consequence' to their overture. Even young infants are not passive learners. Infants are active in choosing what to attend to, and in engaging the attention of others. When a toddler asks for a particular toy, a carer who responds by giving them the toy and extending the interaction ('Here's teddy. I think he is hungry!') is supporting cognitive development. A carer who *consistently* (not occasionally) ignores the child or responds by saying 'Be quiet. You don't need that now' is not supporting cognitive development. A child who is consistently neglected or ignored or treated without warmth is at risk for impaired social, cognitive, and academic outcomes.

As well as warm and responsive caretaking, a key factor for child development is *language*. Both the quality and the quantity of language matter. The child's brain is a learning machine, and the brain requires sufficient *input* to learn effectively. Studies of toddlers suggest that they hear over 5,000 utterances every day. Indeed, one US study suggested that children living in homes with higher incomes heard on average 487 utterances per hour. In contrast, children in homes with lower incomes heard on average 178 utterances per hour. The authors calculated that by the age of 4 years, the higher-income children had heard about 44 million utterances. The lower-income children had heard about 12 million. Environmental differences like this have very important consequences for the brain. As we will see, the optimal development of grammar (knowledge about language structure) and phonology (knowledge about the sound elements in words) depends on the brain experiencing sufficient linguistic input. So quantity of language matters.

The *quality* of the language used with young children is also important. The easiest way to extend the quality of language is with interactions around books. Even looking at the pictures in a book together and chatting about them will lead to the use of more complex grammatical forms and the introduction of novel concepts. The language needed for simple caretaking activities is not very complex, although it is important for cementing routines.

Interacting with books every day with a child automatically introduces more complex language, and consequently provides an enormous stimulus to cognitive development. Indeed, studies show that the richness of language input in the early years has effects not just on later intellectual skills, but also on emotional skills such as resolving conflicts with peers.

Natural conversations, focused on real events in the here and now, are those which are critical for optimal development. Despite this evidence, just talking to young children is still not valued strongly in many environments. Some studies find that over 60 per cent of utterances to young children are 'empty language'—phrases such as 'stop that', 'don't go there', and 'leave that alone'. Obviously, such phrases can be a necessary part of daily interactions with a young child. However, studies of children who experience high levels of such 'restricted language' reveal a negative impact on later cognitive, social, and academic development. Effective caretakers use language to support and 'scaffold' the child's activities. For example, a child might be stirring a puddle with a stick. Rather than saying 'Stop doing that, you'll get dirty!', a carer could say 'Are you using the stick to stir that puddle? Look at the circles you are making. Can you make the circles go round the other way? Yes, good job!' Such a response extends the 'learning environment' around the *child's* chosen focus of attention.

When reading the rest of this book, keep in mind that the child is an *active* learner, not a passive learner. If children experience early learning environments at home, at nursery, and in school that are warm, responsively contingent, and linguistically rich, then the young brain will have the best opportunity for optimal development. These learning environments support all the amazing cognitive and social capacities that develop so rapidly in all infants and children. I shall discuss some of these capacities in the rest of this book.

Chapter 1
Babies and what they know

Early learning

The baby's brain starts to learn inside the womb. By the third trimester (months 6–9), the infant can hear their mother's voice. Indeed, despite the filtering effect of the amniotic fluid, at birth babies can distinguish their mother's voice from that of a strange female. This was shown by a famous 'sucking' experiment, in which newborn babies were given a dummy to suck. First, their natural or 'baseline' sucking rate was measured. Next, the infants were played a tape recording of their mother reading a story. Each time their suck rate increased above baseline, the tape would play. Each time the suck rate dropped below baseline, a strange female voice would be heard instead, reading the same story. The infants rapidly learned to suck fast to hear their mother's voice. The following day, the experimenters reversed the contingency. Now *slower* sucking was required to hear their mother's voice—and the babies reversed their suck rates. Similar 'sucking' experiments have been done using story reading. Mothers read a particular story every day to their 'bump' during the final trimester. At birth, the infants could distinguish the familiar story from a novel story. Indeed, sucking experiments have even shown that infants can learn music inside the womb. Infants whose mothers were fans of the soap opera *Neighbours* were able to recognize the *Neighbours* theme tune at birth.

Babies also move a lot inside the womb. Even by the 15th week, the foetus can use a number of distinct movement patterns. These include a 'yawn and stretch' position and a 'stepping' pattern used for self-rotation. Aspects of the intra-uterine environment, such as the regular heartbeat of the mother, also seem to be learned, and can subsequently have a soothing effect. Studies have shown heartrate deceleration in the foetus in response to certain sounds (thought to index attention). They have also shown habituation (lack of change) of heart rate to familiar stimuli, thought to indicate learning. Therefore, foetal studies show that the infant brain is already learning, remembering, and attending, even inside the womb.

Most of the brain cells that comprise the brain are actually formed before birth. Because of this, if the *environment* inside the womb contains excessive toxins, such as excessive alcohol or drugs (i.e. alcoholism or drug addiction, not the odd glass of wine), this will affect brain development. These effects are not reversible, although the environment that is experienced following birth can remediate negative effects to some extent. The brain itself remains plastic throughout the life of the individual. However, plasticity is largely achieved by the brain growing connections between brain cells that are already there. *Any environmental input* will cause new connections to form. At the same time, connections that are not used much will be pruned. Therefore, no single experience can have disastrous developmental consequences. On the other hand, the *consistency* of what is experienced will be important in determining which connections are pruned and which are retained. If a child consistently experiences warmth and love, different connections will be strengthened compared to a child who consistently experiences anxiety and fear.

One reason that the early years are so important is that the brain is in effect a machine for learning. The brain cells are ready to go even before birth. They also have certain inbuilt ways of processing information, which research has uncovered. The early capability of this learning machine determines the efficiency of later learning. At birth, brains are not so different. They all have the same inbuilt ways of processing information. However, a brain that is offered early advantages can develop its early architecture more efficiently. So a brain that is born into an optimal learning environment will do better over a person's lifetime than a brain that is faced with a less optimal early environment. On the other hand, the malleability of the early brain means that interventions can always have an effect. Interventions, such as changing an environment (e.g., by being fostered), can support the strengthening of the connections that process information more optimally or efficiently. This is particularly the case during the first few years of life. So improving a child's environment will always have a positive effect on later developmental outcomes.

Finally, there are always *individual differences* between brains. At birth, individual differences are primarily in sensory processing (such as the efficiency of neural mechanisms for seeing or hearing) and lability (fussiness, or speed to respond to stimuli). It is the *environment* that will determine whether these individual differences, which characterize all of us, have trivial or more measurable consequences. Brains whose biology makes them less efficient in particular and measurable aspects of processing seem to be at risk in specific areas of development. For example, when auditory processing is less efficient, this can carry a risk of later language impairment. Individual differences are not deterministic: less efficiency does not automatically mean a developmental impairment. Usually, as long as the environment is rich enough, sufficient learning experiences enable less efficient brains to reach similar developmental end points to more efficient brains. However, early awareness of impaired efficiency can enable useful environmental interventions. An extreme example is deafness. In some cases of deafness, a small microchip (called a cochlear implant) can be inserted close to the ear in infancy, and for some cochlear implant children, oral language development is then as good as for hearing children.

Further, even identical twins who developed from the same egg will have different brains. It is not yet clear why this is. One possibility is that these individual differences may depend on the environment inside the womb, which will be experienced slightly differently by each baby. One twin is usually dominant, so perhaps always changes their position first. The other twin must then accommodate this change by changing their position. So the second twin has a different intra-uterine experience to the first twin. Nevertheless, identical twin research shows that biology is never destiny (see Chapter 7). The environment will always have a major impact on child development. The environments in which children develop are governed by their families, their nurseries and schools, and wider society.

People, faces, and eyes

Other people are by far the most interesting things in the world of the baby. Research shows that infants are fascinated by faces from birth. Indeed, there is a specialized brain system for face processing, which seems to function in the same way in infants and adults. Experiments with neonates and young infants show that faces are always preferred over other stimuli, particularly live, mobile faces. The eyes are especially interesting. Newborn infants prefer to look at faces with eyes gazing directly at them. They dislike looking at faces with eyes that are averted. Babies also react negatively to a 'still face'—an experimental situation in which the mother deliberately suspends interaction with the baby and just looks blank. Presented with a 'still face', babies become fussy and upset and look away. The 'still face'—maternal unresponsiveness—also causes elevated levels of the stress hormone cortisol for some babies. Mothers who are clinically depressed show features of 'still face' behaviour.

Some psychological theories argue that *social rejection* is the most powerful form of psychological suffering. For example, Philippe Rochat (2009) suggests that infants' upset reaction to a 'still face' is early evidence for the importance of social interaction in forming a concept of the self. According to these 'socio-cultural' theories of child development, our 'self' is defined by how others react to us. If others are positive to us and interact warmly with us, we feel good about ourselves. If others are hostile or ignoring, we feel bad about ourselves. Socio-cultural theories also argue that our need to avoid social separation and rejection (e.g., avoiding bullying and punishment) determines much of our behaviour. We all need social proximity and intimacy. The forms of proximity and intimacy offered by our environments determine how we think about who we are.

Newborn infants will also imitate facial gestures made by adults. This suggests that babies are intuitively aware of their own bodies. Babies are also immediately engaged by what other people are doing. In one famous study carried out in a maternity hospital (see Figure 1), infants aged from 1 hour old imitated an adult who was either opening his mouth or sticking out his tongue. To test imitation experimentally, the infants were tested in a dark room with their mothers. A light would come on and illuminate the experimenter's face. He either stuck out his tongue, or opened his mouth wide. After 20 seconds, the light went out, and the infant was filmed in the dark. The infants stuck out their tongues more after watching tongue protrusion, and opened their mouths wide more after watching mouth opening.

The capacity to imitate is probably underpinned by a brain system called the 'mirror neuron' system. 'Mirror neuron' brain cells are involved in matching actions to feelings. Mirror neurons are active both when you are watching someone else do something, and when you are doing the same action yourself. For example, the same brain cells are active if you pick up a stick, or if you watch someone else pick up a stick. Therefore, this brain system is thought to be one basis for a shared or 'common code' between the self and others. In order to copy an observed gesture in the dark, babies must be able to map the actions of someone else onto their

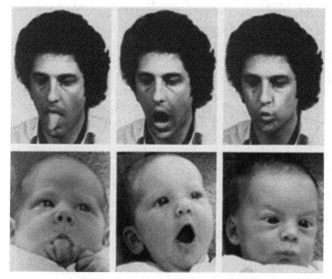

1. Even new-born babies can imitate adult facial gestures

own bodies. This means that they are recognizing that another person is somehow 'like me'. This was shown experimentally by demonstrating that infants do *not* imitate actions made by animated robots. They are apparently aware that a robot is not a human agent. Older infants also imitate people's actions that were never completed successfully. For example, a baby might watch someone trying to put a string of beads into a jar, and yet always missing the jar's opening. When the baby is allowed to play with the beads, they are put straight into the jar. This shows that babies are aware of the *intentions* of other humans. They are not simply imitating their exact physical movements.

Communicative intentions

Intrinsic interest in people's faces and eyes has been linked to how infants are able to acquire language. The argument is that the ability to recognize *intentions* is of central importance. When we speak to someone, we intend them to understand our meaning. Newborn babies have a number of abilities that help them to recognize the 'communicative intentions' of others.

First, babies like direct eye gaze. Even for adults, when someone is looking directly into your eyes and establishing eye contact, this is a signal that you are both 'on line' for talking. Secondly, babies can take turns. All conversation involves turn-taking, and breast feeding is the prototypical turn-taking experience. Both breastfeeding and bottle feeding are characterized by the infant sucking and stopping. When the baby stops, the mother jiggles the infant, who then starts sucking again. Pausing is *not* dependent on needing to breathe or on being full—babies could suck continuously if they wanted to. And jiggling never occurs while the baby is sucking. In fact, the research shows that jiggling doesn't affect the total amount of milk that is taken. Nevertheless, sucking and jiggling are done in turns. This is like the turn-taking pattern of human conversation.

Thirdly, infants are able to detect contingencies. They are aware from very early that some events are intrinsically related (or contingent upon) each other. Sucking and jiggling during breast- or bottle-feeding is one example of 'contingent responsivity'. Each action is contingent upon the occurrence of the other action. Contingent responsivity is an essential property of human interaction, and is an important concept in child psychology. Contingent responding by caretakers promotes healthy psychological development. There are many examples of infants' recognition of contingency. For example, one clever study filmed babies kicking (young babies spend a lot of time kicking). The babies were then given a choice of two films to watch. One film showed their own legs kicking in real time. The other film also showed their own legs, but with a time delay. So in the second film, there was no contingency or intrinsic link between what the infants could feel their legs doing, and what they could see. The experimenters found that babies preferred to watch the contingent video.

Finally, carers tend to use a special tone of voice to talk to babies. This is more sing-song and attention-grabbing than normal conversational speech, and is called 'infant-directed speech' or 'Parentese'. All adults and children naturally adopt this special tone when talking to a baby, and babies prefer to listen to Parentese. For example, when given a choice between listening to tapes of an adult speaking versus the same adult speaking in Parentese, babies will choose to activate the tape that uses Parentese. These are the four critical abilities that seem to be foundational for acquiring language. When someone is gazing directly at you, speaking in Parentese, responding to your gurgling and taking turns with you, these are all signals that you are being intentionally addressed. And they are signals recognized by babies from birth.

Attachment and security

The ability to recognize communicative intent is only one of the intrinsic abilities (or predispositions) towards social interaction that is present in newborn babies. Other innate behaviours such as *rooting* for the breast, *crying* and *grasping* all create proximity to the caretaker. These actions ensure the physical closeness required to build a relationship. Some research suggests that the pitch and amplitude (loudness) of a baby's cry has been developed by evolution to prompt immediate action by adults. Babies' cries appear to be designed to be maximally stressful to hear. Smiling also begins early, and infants use smiles to reward social interaction from carers. Experiments show that infants smile most during *face-to-face contingent* interactions with carers. These are interactions characterized by turn-taking, infant-directed speech and playful warmth ('interpersonal contingency'). At birth infants prefer the mother's voice and the mother's smell, as these are most familiar. However, the important factors in becoming a 'preferred attachment figure' are proximity and consistency. Babies quickly learn to prefer the faces, voices and smells of their most consistent and warm caretakers. These specific attachments that babies form are very important for healthy psychological development.

Nevertheless, research does *not* suggest that separation from the mother following birth (for example, for a medical procedure) prevents 'bonding' with the infant. The psychological relationship or 'bond' that mothers and other caretakers form with infants grows over time. Consistency of contact, responsiveness and warmth are the key attributes. The consistency of early attachment experiences are critical for the development of children's 'internal working models' (psychological expectations) of their value as a person who is deserving of love and support from others. If these interactions are characterized by consistency and warmth, the baby is described as showing 'security of attachment'. If an infant consistently experiences caretaking that fails to be contingent on their needs, or that is not characterized by warmth, then the attachment is said to be 'insecure'. Similarly, if an infant consistently experiences caretaking that is erratic and neglectful, so that sometimes caretaking is contingent on their needs and sometimes it ignores those needs, attachment is also insecure. Infants who are insecurely attached to their caregivers still prefer those caregivers over other people. The term 'insecure attachment' refers to the fact that the infant cannot *rely* on those caregivers responding appropriately to their cries and smiles—or responding at all.

When attachment is insecure, children develop different 'internal working models' of the self. Two main types of insecure attachment are identified in the literature. 'Insecure-avoidant' infants appear to become resigned to their fate. They develop self-protective strategies, such as not seeking contact when the carer is close, as though to protect themselves against disappointment. 'Insecure-dependent' infants become very clingy and fight against separation, as though trying to force appropriate caretaking behaviours from the adult. Research shows that both forms of insecure attachment are related to less positive developmental outcomes long-term. These include social–emotional outcomes, relating to self-esteem and self-control, and also cognitive outcomes, relating to intellectual and academic achievement.

In extreme cases, usually involving parental reactions that are frightening for the infant, attachment is 'disorganized'. Caretaking is so unpredictable that an infant cannot find a way of organizing her behaviour to get her needs met. The internal working model developed in response to such caretaking is often that the child is flawed in some way, and does not deserve love and support from others. Such children are at risk for mental health disorders, including depression, oppositional–defiant disorders or conduct disorders. Healthy attachment relationships do not have to be with the genetic parents. Relationships depend on *learning*. Learning that your social overtures will be met with contingent responsiveness and warmth are the key factors required for babies to develop secure attachments. Grandparents, foster parents and older siblings can all be sources of secure attachments.

Expectations about behaviour

As well as being predisposed to be social, babies also have interesting expectations about how people should behave to each other. Research shows that older babies (around 12 months) expect people to *help others* and to behave *fairly*. For example, in one study infants were shown videos of animated geometric shapes on a computer screen. The shapes moved in certain ways. The screen had a line rising across it, which could be seen as a 'hill' to be 'climbed'. One shape (a circle) duly began to move up this hill. At first it climbed steadily, but then the incline steepened, and the circle rolled back to rest on a plateau. At this point in the video, one of two other shapes (visible at the top of the screen) began to move. For example, a triangle came down to a position behind the circle, and then they moved together to the top of the hill ('helping' scenario). Alternatively, a square came down to a position in front of the circle, and they moved together back to the bottom of the hill ('hindering' scenario). Babies were then allowed to choose between 3D soft toys in the shape of the triangle and the square. The babies all preferred to play with the triangle.

This is only one example of a remarkable series of experiments using moving shapes without eyes that are nonetheless interpreted by watching infants as behaving socially. Indeed, adding eyes to the animations, or using real actors, only enhances the experimental effects. Certain types of motion-based interactions between objects seem to specify social behaviour to the infant brain. Socio-moral expectations in babies can also be revealed by experiments using real objects on a small 'stage'. Infants watch the scenes on stage while sitting on a parent's lap, and hidden experimenters manipulate the 'behaviour' and 'experiences' of the objects. For example, one experiment on socio-moral expectations involved two identical toy giraffes. Each giraffe had a place mat in front of them. As the infant watched, the experimenter showed the giraffes two toys (saying excitedly 'I have toys!'). The giraffes became excited in turn—via hidden means, they began dancing, and shouting 'yay, yay'. The experimenter then either put both toys on the mat in front of one giraffe, or gave the giraffes one toy each. The giraffes looked down at their place mats without reacting. The experimenters recorded how long the babies watched each scene. The babies looked significantly longer at the event which was unfair.

These experiments, which have various control conditions to rule out other explanations of infant's choices or looking times, suggest that some *socio-moral norms* may be innate and culturally universal. Early emerging norms appear to include a concern for fairness, a preference for helping over hindering, and a distaste for actions that harm others. Theoretically, it is thought that socio-moral expectations are inborn because they have evolved to support the continued existence of the species. They are necessary for social group living (society) to work. Socio-moral expectations facilitate positive interactions between people and foster co-operation within social groups.

Clearly, these norms will be elaborated in different ways by different cultures. Further, once language is acquired (see Chapter 3), we can explain to children how they should behave in certain settings, and why certain moral norms are important. However, even the preverbal infant is learning a lot about socio-moral norms by watching the interactions of those around them. This learning appears to be guided by their innate expectations of how people should behave.

The experiences that promote the learning of socio-moral norms clearly overlap with the experiences supporting secure attachment. The main learning environment for both types of experience in early life is *family interactions*. Families in which people have warm and supportive relationships with each other are also likely to be families where there is fairness, helping of each other, and little punitive behaviour. Families in which people have hostile and abusive relationships with each other will present babies with learning experiences that seldom model fairness and helping each other, and may actively model aggressive behaviour. In family settings involving physical abuse, infants may learn to inhibit their innate socio-moral expectations and replace them with other expectations about how people behave to each other.

There is little research on the effects of these more negative learning environments, partly as it is more difficult to involve such families in research. Importantly, these influences on learning will be present *pre-verbally*, and so their effects will be subliminal. The developing infant has no means at their disposal of explaining to themselves the features of their environment. Rather, the environment of the family is their *norm*. The early learning environment offered by the family has profound effects on psychological and social development, on intellectual development and on the internal working model of the self.

Imitation

When infants watch the actions of other people, they also learn about psychological causation. The ability to imitate the actions of others provides a 'like me' analogy. Brain systems like the mirror neuron system do not simply link seeing and producing certain acts. They also link 'that looks the way this feels'. Babies seem to assume that people have *goals*. If babies can understand someone's goal, they can also imitate an unsuccessful action. An example is the 'putting the beads into the jar' experiment discussed earlier. Babies can also imitate selectively depending on the context in which an action occurs. In a famous study, babies watched adults making a completely novel action which they had never seen before. This was to use the forehead to turn on an experimental light panel. The adults made the panel light up by bending forwards and touching it with their heads. Subsequently, the babies were given the light panel to play with. The babies also leaned forward and lit it by using their foreheads. However, babies who watched the same event presented in the context of an adult who was feeling cold, and who had her hands under a shawl, did not use their foreheads to activate the light panel. They just pressed it with their hands. This experiment and others suggest that preverbal infants can infer psychological goals.

Experiments like these show that infants can recognize other people's intentions, and will imitate accordingly. Further, infants will not imitate accidental actions. Babies also discriminate between an actor who intends to give them a desired toy, but fails (because she cannot get it out of its box), and an actor who can get the toy out of the box, but chooses not to give the toy to the baby. This suggests an insight into the *hidden mental states* governing the adult's actions (importantly, the baby does not get the toy in either case). The babies reached out for the toy more and banged the table in frustration more when the actor chose not to pass over the toy than when the actor was unable to give them the toy. This shows an emergent understanding of psychological causation. Furthermore, the recognition of what people intend is important for effective learning. If babies only imitate the intentional acts of others, then they will acquire many significant cultural skills.

Joint attention

The imitiation experiments suggest that infants are not 'mind blind'. Infants are not unaware of the hidden mental causes of people's actions. Although some researchers still dispute this, it appears that babies make mentalistic assumptions that the actions of other people have psychological causes. Babies also interpret *seeing* as an intentional act. From a young age, babies will follow gaze. They seem to be aware that we look at things because we are getting information about them. Babies able to crawl, who see an adult gazing excitedly at something hidden by a screen, will move to a position where they can see what is being looked at. By around 8–10 months of age, preverbal babies will also try and direct the attention of someone else to something interesting. They do this by pointing at it. Developmentally, there are two kinds of pointing—pointing at something because you wish to be given it, and pointing at something simply to share attention with someone else. The second kind of pointing, which becomes very frequent from around 10 months onwards, is intended by the baby to influence the mental state of another person. This kind of pointing has *communicative intent*. Interestingly, the absence of this kind of pointing by babies is an early indicator of risk for autism.

Joint attention to an object is a key developmental advance. It is a clear indicator that infants are aware of the mental states of other people. Joint attention is about communicating and sharing experiences. Theoretically, when the child points in order to engage someone's attention, the child is sharing his or her psychological state with that person ('I am interested in this'). The child is also showing an awareness of *normative behaviour* ('This is the kind of thing *we* like to share psychologically, because we are in the same group').

Joint attention has also been suggested to be the basis of 'natural pedagogy'—a social learning system for imparting cultural knowledge. Once attention is shared by adult and infant on an object, an interaction around that object can begin. That interaction usually passes knowledge from carer to child. This is an example of responsive contingency in action—the infant shows an interest in something, the carer responds, and there is an interaction which enables learning. Taking the *child's focus of attention* as the starting point for the interaction is very important for effective learning. Of course, skilled carers can also engineer situations in which babies or children will become interested in certain objects. This is the basis of effective play-centred learning. Novel toys or objects are always interesting. Objects in which adults show consistent interest are also interesting to infants—for example, car keys and mobile telephones!

Babies will also monitor adults or other children for signs to tell them how they should react to something novel. Again, this suggests an insight into the mental states of others. Such monitoring, called 'social referencing', has been shown in various experimental settings. For example, one set of experiments used a mildly scary mechanical robot called 'Magic Mike'. The experiment used a joint attention setting, in which mothers were trained to look either frightened or happy when Magic Mike appeared. The mothers also used an appropriately emotional tone of voice to say either 'How frightful' or 'How delightful' (the phrases were deliberately chosen to sound similar but be unfamiliar). In the fearful setting, infants did not approach Magic Mike and also became upset themselves. In the happy setting, infants behaved no differently compared to a 'neutral face' setting, in which mothers were neutral. In both the happy and neutral cases, the infants approached Magic Mike and played with him.

2. A baby on the visual cliff

The most famous social referencing studies in child psychology began in the 1960s and involved a 'visual cliff', shown in Figure 2. Babies who could crawl were placed on a Perspex table top. The Perspex surface covered a design of black and white squares, which were on a surface much lower than the Perspex in the horizontal plane. The squares varied in size to manipulate visual cues to depth, giving the visual impression of a sudden drop. The experiments showed that babies would crawl to the edge of the 'cliff' and then look at their mothers for guidance. If the mother looked fearful, most of the babies went no further.

The social brain

These varied experiments on imitation, joint attention, and socio-moral expectations show that infants and toddlers are developing psychological understanding from very early indeed. There is emerging awareness of the mental states of others much earlier than was traditionally believed. Freud, for example, thought that infants were not aware of the *self–other* distinction. He argued that physical birth was not the same as psychological birth. Some types of experiment seemed to reinforce these classical ideas of early 'mindblindness'. Behaviour with mirrors, for example, does not always suggest that young children are aware that it is them in the mirror. On one hand, experiments show that children as young as 3–5 months will test out mirrors by moving different parts of their bodies and seeing what happens in the mirror. On the other hand, it is not until the age of 18 months that children will pass the 'mark test'. In the mark test, a red mark is surreptitiously put on the child's face. The test is whether children will touch the mark when they see themselves in the mirror. Many children do not. This behaviour may suggest that consciousness of the self develops gradually. However, it may also be linked to the experimental situation, and as yet remains poorly understood.

A critical factor in early developing psychological awareness is the fact that the infant's caretakers treat him or her as a *social partner*. Indeed, carers probably treat infants as acting socially even before infants are deliberately acting in this way. The human brain is a social brain, because humans are a social species. Babies are innately predisposed to be with other humans and maintain social closeness.

As already noted, high quality care does not have to be from the biological parent to be effective. This is further supported by research on daycare settings. Recent studies have employed an objective measure of stress, the hormone *cortisol*, to assess how much stress preverbal children experience in different types of care settings. Cortisol is measured in the saliva, and higher levels of cortisol are associated with higher levels of stress. Children in high-quality learning environments show lower cortisol levels in these studies, whether they are cared for at home or in a nursery. In high-quality daycare settings, carers provide focused attention and warm stimulation that is essentially sensitive parenting (i.e., warm and responsively contingent). In such settings, cortisol levels are low. In low-quality learning environments, where carers are intrusive and over-controlling and lack warmth, cortisol levels are high. Again, this is true whether the carer is the biological parent, a nanny or a nursery care assistant.

Accordingly, good teachers, nannies, and daycare providers act as figures of secure attachment. They provide early learning environments that are very similar to high-quality home environments. The best of all worlds is to experience a high-quality learning environment both at home and at nursery. Recent studies suggest that children in high-quality daycare who also have secure attachments to their families show the optimal cortisol profile when in their daycare settings.

Chapter 2
Learning about the outside world

Nature versus nurture

Before they can talk and ask questions, babies and toddlers learn a remarkable amount about the world from looking and listening. Some child psychologists believe that this enormously rapid learning is possible because certain concepts, or ways of interpreting information, are *innate*. Even if this view is wrong, and there is no innate knowledge about the world present in the brain at birth, babies certainly learn about the world very fast indeed. Further, the kinds of information that they learn appears to be 'constrained'. Some types of information are learned more easily. For example, causal relations appear to be learned particularly easily by babies. This may suggest that certain aspects of the external world are *prioritized* for learning. Internal 'constraints on learning' would govern these priorities, helping to determine the objects and events that babies give their attention to. Another possibility is that these *constraints on learning* are imposed by the way that neural sensory systems acquire and process information. For example, movement is very salient to the visual system. So perhaps an early focus on how objects move is driven in part by the number of motion-sensitive neurons (brain cells) present, and the kinds of input the visual system requires for further development.

Another, complementary possibility is that adults modify their actions in important ways when they interact with infants. These modifications appear to facilitate learning. 'Infant-directed action' is characterized by greater enthusiasm, closer proximity to the infant, greater repetitiveness, and longer gaze to the face than interactions with another adult. Infant-directed action also uses simplified actions with more turn-taking. For example, in representative studies a mother might be filmed demonstrating an object to her baby and then demonstrating the same object to her partner. When other babies are subsequently given a choice of which film to watch, they systematically prefer to watch the films of infant-directed actions. These spontaneous action patterns, also called 'motionese', hence serve to increase the baby's attention to what is taking place. The action patterns also signal that 'this behaviour is relevant to you'. Such studies show that infants are not passive learners. Instead of simply processing everything in the visual field, infants *select* which actions to watch.

Active not passive learners

Research shows that all the looking and listening that babies do is organized mentally into certain types of knowledge from early in life. Listening to and looking at people teaches babies about how people behave ('naive psychology'). Listening to and looking at objects and events teaches babies about how the external physical world operates. Babies learn what objects are like (e.g., rigid or flexible), and how objects move, and they learn the distinction between 'natural kinds' (animals and plants) and 'artefacts' (things made by man). Learning about objects is 'naive physics', while learning about the natural world is 'naive biology'. Young babies are already developing at least three types of knowledge that map onto distinctions that are still made at university level—psychology, physics, and biology.

Indeed, one popular theoretical approach in child psychology is to draw an analogy between infants and scientists. The premise is that babies and scientists have a similar approach to learning. Both babies and scientists make observations, carry out experiments, and draw conclusions. A baby who keeps dropping the same toy for her mother to retrieve is learning the relationship between cause and effect ('I drop, you fetch'). She is also learning about the different trajectories that the toy can fall along, and indirectly, she is learning about gravity ('objects always fall if they are released, and they fall straight down'). The 'baby as scientist' approach argues that infants have naive *theories* about how the world works. These theories are claimed to be based on innate expectations.

The kind of innate expectations (or 'principles' or 'constraints' guiding learning) are expectations like 'one thing cannot be in two places at the same time'. These innate expectations are then elaborated via learning—looking, listening, smelling, feeling, and tasting. For example, while one thing can never be in two places at once, two things can be in one place at once. This is possible if one object is inside another (the physical concept of *containment*).

An important milestone in learning about objects comes when babies are able to grasp efficiently. Once babies can manipulate things by themselves, learning really takes off. Indeed, a clever set of experiments using 'sticky mittens' with very young babies (3-month-olds) showed that being able to handle objects significantly accelerated learning. Usually, the ability to grasp objects unaided begins at around 4 months. As the 'sticky mittens' had Velcro on them, soft toys stuck to the 3-month-old babies' hands. Hence these younger babies could experience making a range of different actions on the toys. The 'sticky mitten' babies subsequently showed earlier understanding of the actions of an adult who was reaching for objects. This was measured in comparison to other babies of 3 months, who simply watched the same toys being manipulated by someone else. So initiating actions *oneself* is important for effective learning.

Another important milestone is being able to sit up unsupported. This usually occurs between 4 and 6 months of age. Being able to sit upright enables babies to expand their range of actions on the world. For example, babies can now turn objects around and turn them upside down. They can feel textures, see the objects from different angles, and pass them from hand to hand (note that 'baby gym' toys offer prone babies similar learning opportunities). Becoming a 'self-sitter' has been shown to be related to babies' understanding of objects as being three dimensional.

Perhaps an even more important developmental milestone is being able to move by yourself. Crawling and then walking enables the baby to get to the places she wants to go. While crawling makes it difficult to carry objects with you on your travels, learning to walk enables babies to carry things. Indeed, walking babies spend most of their time selecting objects and taking them to show their carer, spending on average 30–40 minutes per waking hour interacting with objects. Even though an expert crawler can move more quickly and efficiently than a novice walker, babies persevere in learning to walk. Walking usually develops between 11 and 12 months in Western cultures, and babies practise hard. One study showed that newly walking infants take over 2,000 steps per hour, covering the length of approximately seven football pitches. The average distance travelled of 700 metres each hour means that during an average waking day, and allowing for meals, bathtime, etc., most infants are travelling over 5 kilometres!

Self-generated movement is seen as critical for child development. Being able to crawl and then to walk enables babies to go to the places that *they* choose. The babies can then initiate object-focused social interactions. As we all know, the places that babies choose include a number of places that adults do not want them to visit, like stairs, fireplaces, and plug sockets. Indeed, research shows that novice walkers can have very bad judgement even with respect to choosing which path to follow. For example, babies will hesitate at the top of a steep slope for ages, but then plunge down headfirst nonetheless. Or babies will dangle their foot into a gap that they cannot cross, then try anyway, and fall. Nevertheless, most falling is *adaptive*, as it helps infants to gain expertise. Indeed, studies show that newly walking infants fall on average 17 times per hour.

From the perspective of child psychology, the importance of 'motor milestones' like crawling and walking is that they enable greater *agency* (self-initiated and self-chosen behaviour) on the part of the baby. Like the scientist, the baby can now intervene in events, and see what happens next. Annoying examples of the 'baby as scientist' include unplugging the Hoover during hoovering, and manipulating the buttons on the TV or DVD unobserved, thereby changing the settings.

Memory and attention

Although young babies may appear to be rather unaware of the world around them, in fact both memory and attention are functioning from very early indeed. Very young babies (younger than 6 weeks) can have trouble deliberately following objects with their eyes, but even newborns can attend to objects and can see the whole visual scene (not just blobs of colour and light). Very young babies like looking at displays that have lots of visual contrast. For example, they like looking at displays with clear black and white divisions, like chessboard patterns. Some cot mobiles use black-and-white patterning for this reason. One possibility is that visual scenes with maximal contrast between light and dark areas help the brain's visual system to develop expertise in seeing. Edge detection and motion detection are key components of how vision works. In fact, sometimes younger babies can find it difficult to *stop* paying attention to certain objects—so-called 'sticky fixation'. Babies might even start crying when they cannot move their gaze. This usually solves the problem, as usually the infant will then get picked up or moved, and gaze is broken.

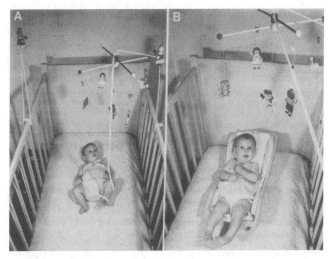

3. Testing infant memory using cot mobiles

A nice example of early memory and attention comes from some famous experiments using cot mobiles. Babies who are lying on their backs in a cot spend a lot of time kicking. To create an experiment, researchers tied a ribbon to the babies' ankles, shown in Figure 3. At first, the ribbon was just tied to a stand, and so kicking didn't cause anything to happen. Once a 'baseline' kick rate was established, the experimenters tied the ribbon to an interesting cot mobile instead. The mobile moved and made musical sounds. Babies rapidly learned to kick at an increased rate to activate the mobile. A few days later, the babies were put back in the cot with the same novel mobile. Kicking was again measured, although this time the mobile did not activate. Babies of 3 months still kicked much more compared to their baseline kick rate. This suggested that they retained a *memory* of the cause–effect relationship.

In fact, extra kicking, the index of remembering, could be demonstrated over gaps as long as two weeks. When given a 'reminder' of the contingency (for example, the mobile was activated briefly before the ribbon was tied to the ankle), these very young babies showed memories over gaps as long as a month. In experimental situations like the mobile situation, the 'learning event' (i.e., activating the mobile by kicking) is a one-off event. It is only experienced one time, yet the babies learn and remember it. In everyday life, of course, babies will experience contingencies or cause–effect relations on a daily basis. So infant memory is likely to be even better than these experiments suggest.

One persuasive test of the persistence of early memories was carried out by a research team in the USA. They decided to bring back as 2-and-a-half-year-olds children who had participated in an experiment on sound localization as 6-month-old babies. In this *sound localization* experiment, the 6-month-old babies had been required to reach in the dark for a Big Bird puppet that made a rattling sound. Two years later, the children came back to the same experimental room, met the same female experimenter, and were shown some toys, including the Big Bird toy. They then had to reach in the dark. The children showed clear 'implicit' memory of their experiences at 6 months. They were significantly faster and more accurate at reaching for Big Bird compared to other 2-and-a-half-year-olds, who had not experienced the set-up when aged 6 months. In fact, when given a 'reminder' of their early experience (hearing the rattle sound for three seconds, half an hour before being asked to reach in the dark), these children were even faster to reach in the dark.

This is good evidence for long-term memories forming as early as 6 months. Like adults, children also do better in memory tasks when given hints or reminders. Another indicator of implicit memory was that most of the 2-and-half-year-olds did not find the 'dark reaching' experiment distressing. In contrast, over half of the control children (those who had not reached in the dark as 6-month-olds) didn't enjoy sitting in the dark, and asked to stop before the experiment was completed.

Cross-modal sensory knowledge and early numerosity

Young babies are also aware of objects in many modalities. For example, as adults we can usually tell what an object will feel like from looking at it. We are surprised when, for example, an object that appears to be a rock turns out to be a sponge. Babies as young as 1 month also seem to make connections *across* sensory modalities. This was shown in an experiment involving a dummy which had a nubbled surface. Babies were given one of two dummies to suck, either the nubbled dummy or a smooth dummy. The experimenters made sure that the babies didn't see the dummy as it went into their mouths. This meant that the babies had only *tactile experience* of the dummy. Babies were then given pictures of both dummies to look at. The babies consistently preferred to look at the dummy that they had just been sucking. Babies who had sucked the nubbled dummy gazed at this picture, and babies who had sucked the smooth dummy gazed at this picture.

In fact, multisensory understanding in infancy has been demonstrated in a variety of ways. In an experiment using videos, babies were given a choice of watching either two 'talking heads' or three 'talking heads'. The videos showed either two or three female experimenters looking at the baby and mouthing the word 'look'. The sound of either two or three different voices all saying 'look' at the same time was then played from a central speaker. When they could hear two voices, the babies looked at the video of two women. When they could hear three voices, they looked at the video of three women. As well as showing multisensory insight, this experiment also suggests early sensitivity to number—that three is more than two.

Number is another cognitive system that has been thought to be partly innate. For example, babies as young as 5 months seem to be able to add and subtract small numbers. In these number experiments, babies watched events unfold on a small stage while sitting on a parent's lap. As they watched the empty stage, a hand from the side put a Mickey Mouse doll centre-stage. A screen at the front of the stage then rotated up and covered Mickey from view. As the infant watched, the hand appeared again at the side of the stage and added a second Mickey Mouse doll to the hidden area behind the screen. When the screen was lowered, the watching infant saw either two dolls or a single Mickey Mouse doll. Two dolls was the expected outcome, but one doll was wrong—because $1 + 1 = 2$. Infants looked for much longer at the single doll than at two dolls. Babies also showed similar reactions to a *subtraction* version of the event. In the subtraction version, two dolls were hidden by the screen and one doll was then removed in view of the infant. If the screen was lowered and two dolls were still present, infants looked for much longer than if the screen was lowered to reveal a single doll. This early evidence for a 'number sense' has been argued to show that there is an innate brain system for representing small numbers. Babies perform well in these kinds of experiments with the numbers 1, 2, and 3. After that, they seem to approximate larger numbers as 'many', and operate with an approximate system based on ratio. This is discussed in Chapter 5.

Physical relations between objects

Infants also seem to possess remarkably accurate expectations about physical relations between objects. These are relations like *occlusion*, *containment*, and *support*. Again, the experiments establishing these expectations usually depend on the 'violation of expectation' paradigm. Babies watch events on a small stage while sitting on the parental lap. The mothers and fathers usually wear blindfolds and headphones, so that they cannot inadvertently affect their infant's reaction. These kinds of experiments have shown that babies do not assume that objects disappear if they are hidden from view by other objects that might pass in front of them (occlusion), or by other objects that contain them.

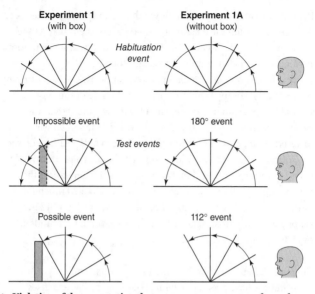

4. Violation of the expectation that a screen cannot rotate through a solid object

In one famous series of violation of expectation experiments, babies watched a stage with a rotating screen, shown in Figure 4. The screen would rotate up from a flat position, eventually hiding whatever object was on the stage, and continuing to rotate until it made contact with the object. If a wooden box was on the stage, and the screen rotated through 180° (impossible event), the babies looked for much longer than if the screen stopped on contact with the box, at 120°. On the other hand, if a sponge of similar dimensions was on the stage, the babies expected a degree of compression. They did not keep staring at the stage if the screen rotated past 120°. In both scenarios, the babies clearly expected that the hidden object continued to exist. Out of sight is not 'out of mind' for babies.

Another set of experiments involved toy cars running on tracks on a stage-like setting. The initial stage set-up showed a toy car at the top of a ramp. A track ran down the ramp and along the stage. A screen was then raised and obscured part of the track. As the babies watched, a toy car at the top of the ramp was set in motion. It ran on the track down the ramp, and then ran along the stage, passing briefly behind the screen, then reappearing and continuing to run until it disappeared from view at the side of the stage. After the babies had watched this event a few times, the screen was raised and an obstacle was put on the track. The screen was then lowered again, and the car was put at the top of the ramp and set in motion. If the babies understood that the obstacle continued to exist behind the screen, then they should no longer expect the car to reappear. Babies as young as 3 months looked much longer at the car event when the car reappeared than when it did not reappear. Again, this suggests that babies assume that hidden objects continue to exist.

Since the invention of brain imaging methods, similar experiments have been done while recording brain responses (EEG—electroencephalography). EEG measures the low-voltage electrical signals that pass between brain cells in response to environmental events. In one EEG experiment, babies watched a toy train chuffing into a tunnel and not reappearing from the other end. The tunnel was then lifted up to reveal the train. The appearance of the train was *expected*—the train had obviously remained in the tunnel. Sometimes, the tunnel was lifted and revealed to be empty, even though the train had not been seen leaving the tunnel. This was an *unexpected* disappearance. On still other occasions, the train chuffed into one side of the tunnel, and chuffed out the other side, and the tunnel was lifted to reveal no train. This was an *expected* disappearance event. The researchers compared babies' brain activity to the two types of disappearance events. Brain activity was quite different in the *expected* disappearance event compared to the *unexpected* disappearance event. Therefore, even though no train was visible in either event, and in both events the baby was gazing at the same empty location, electrical signalling in the brain showed different patterns. The babies also looked significantly longer at the unexpected disappearance event. This experiment suggested that increased looking time is indeed an index of what the babies are *thinking*.

Search behaviour

One reason that psychology experiments have tried to establish whether out of sight is 'out of mind' for babies is that according to one influential theory in child psychology, infants have to *construct* the notion of object permanence, via learning. Jean Piaget (see Chapter 7) suggested that infants did not have a full understanding of the permanent existence of objects until around 18 months of age. One important experiment involved measuring where infants look for objects. Piaget demonstrated that even 10-month-old babies would look in the wrong place for hidden objects. In Piaget's famous 'A-not-B' paradigm, babies watched as an experimenter repeatedly hid a desirable object (like a bunch of keys) under one cloth, 'location A' (shown in Figure 5). After each hiding event, the

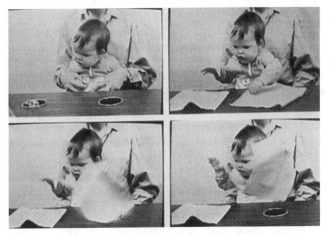

5. A baby searching at location A while fixating location B in the A-not-B paradigm

baby was allowed to retrieve the keys by lifting the cloth. The baby then watched as the experimenter hid the keys under a new cloth, 'location B'. Surprisingly, most babies again lifted cloth A, failing to find the keys. The same error was made when transparent boxes were used for the hiding locations. Even though the keys were visible in box B, the babies would open box A.

A number of different theories have been proposed to explain this search behaviour. One is Piaget's original theory about *immature object knowledge*. Other theories include *brain immaturity*, in which immature connections between different brain systems prevent knowledge about the hiding location (location B) controlling action (reaching to A), and *perseveration of action* (in which the baby fails to inhibit the habitual response of reaching to A). However, perhaps the most interesting recent theory of the A-not-B error points out that babies are *active social partners* in all of our experiments. In the classic A-not-B paradigm, the experimenter is making eye contact with the infant while chatting ('Hello baby, look here'), cues that usually signal 'in this situation, we do this' (i.e., reach to location A). To test this 'teaching' explanation, experimenters created a 'non-social' A-not-B test. Here, the infants watched the two locations A and B while no person was visible (the experimenter sat behind a curtain). A hand slid out from behind the curtain to repeatedly hide the object at location A. After a number of successful retrievals by the infant, the hand slid out and hid the object at location B. This time, on the first B trial, over half of the babies successfully retrieved the hidden object from the new location. Hence in the absence of social cues and when attending only to the *spatial lay-out* of the hiding event, babies are much less likely to search in the wrong location.

Distinguishing biological and non-biological kinds

Babies experience many objects in the environment that move and make a noise, but only some of these have *agency*—self-directed movement. Pets, for example, move around, make noises, and do interesting things. Cars, by contrast, may move around and make noises, but they cannot decide to start moving by themselves. In fact, there are all sorts of physical cues connected to motion that indicate whether something is an *agent* or not. These cues are detected by babies quite early in development.

One series of relevant experiments has used 'point light' displays. Point light displays were first created using people. Experimenters attached small points of light to the major joints and to the head, and then filmed people moving in the dark while dressed in black (shown in Figure 6). The motion of these points of light enabled adults viewing the films to recognize people walking, dancing, doing push-ups or riding a bicycle. Even gender could be determined just from motion. Point light display experiments with infants show that babies can also distinguish walking from random movement, and someone walking upside down. They can also distinguish biological versus non-biological kinds, like cars versus dogs. In the dog/car experiment, some 3-month-old babies saw photographs of cars and dogs, which provided rich perceptual featural information. The babies could easily distinguish the two kinds of photo. Other babies saw just the *motion* associated with different cars or with different dogs. These babies were equally successful at distinguishing the cars from the dogs, even though no other visual features were present. Hence *type of motion* is an important cue for distinguishing agents from man-made artefacts like cars.

Another method for showing that babies can distinguish 'natural kinds' from artefacts relies on 'sequential touching'. Older babies who can sit up and manipulate objects do not touch things indiscriminately. Rather, they touch things systematically. In one demonstration, 12-month-old babies were given a large set of toys, half of which were toy cars and half of which were toy animals. The babies sequentially touched objects from the same category significantly more often that would be expected on the basis of

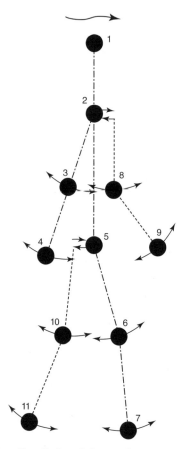

6. A point-light walker display of a human figure

chance. The same 'sequential touching' effect was found even when the toys looked very similar. In one study, wooden toy animals were made that were identical in shape to pieces of toy furniture. The pieces of toy furniture had features like eyes painted on them. Nevertheless, the babies did not behave indiscriminately. For example, if the babies were given a series of animals to manipulate, and were then given a piece of furniture, they spent much longer examining the novel piece of furniture than they spent examining a new animal that had an identical shape. Experiments like these suggest that infants are *categorizing* objects on the basis of their prior knowledge.

Emergent 'essentialist' theories

Theoretically, such research has promoted the idea that even babies have emergent 'theories' about how the world works. Older children (2- and 3-year-olds), like babies, also use deeper, more essential characteristics than perceptual appearance to categorize objects. For example, in one famous experiment 2-year-olds were shown a series of pictures of fairly typical birds who live in nests (robin, sparrow, blackbird). They were then shown a picture of an unfamiliar bird that did not look bird-like, for example a *dodo*. The children were asked 'Does it live in a nest?' Children judged that the dodo would also live in a nest. When shown a picture of a pterodactyl (which looks like a bird, but is a dinosaur), the children judged that it would *not* live in a nest. Hence their categorization behaviour did not rely on perceptual features. Related research suggested that even young children have already learned a number of *principles* relating to category membership, and have organized the natural world according to these principles. Such theories can broadly be called 'psychological essentialism'. These underlying principles or essential characteristics then guide further development.

According to essentialist theories, young children routinely go *beyond* observable features when developing biological concepts. Young children pay attention to causal principles, and they search for causal explanations to make sense of how the world works. The paradigm of 'child as theorist' has also uncovered the principles that children use to categorize artefacts. Again, motion is important, but so is function. Man-made artefacts like furniture are specifically designed to fulfil particular functions. Therefore, children will categorize things with a wide variety of appearances as 'bags' or 'chairs'. As long as an artefact can function as a bag or a chair, it *is* a bag or a chair. Young children also do not expect artefacts to grow, to move by themselves or to have babies. However, they expect biological kinds, like dogs, rabbits and flies, to do all of these things. Even 4-year-olds will say that leaves can change colour on their own, but that guitars cannot play by themselves. Theoretically, it is argued that children develop an understanding of natural cause from a mixture of observation, learning, and an innate tendency to search for hidden features that make things similar—the *essentialist bias*.

The importance of multisensory knowledge

One source of the rich learning evident by age 4 is the brain's ability to detect patterns in all kinds of information. Usually, the behaviour of objects, or the appearance of natural kinds, follows a pattern. The kind of motion typical of a vehicle, for example, will take the pattern of a straight line at a constant speed. A dog or a fly, on the other hand, will move randomly all over the place, changing trajectory and speed at will. Usually, the visual information will be supplemented by related sounds (an engine sound, which is relatively constant, versus a buzzing or running sound, which is not constant), perhaps by related smells, and sometimes by tactile information. Even 2-month-old babies can detect visual or auditory patterns. In one experiment on *statistical learning*, infants watched a stream of coloured geometric shapes presented on a computer screen. The shapes did not occur randomly, but in patterns of pairs (e.g., a blue cross was always followed by a yellow circle). The infants did not just learn which shapes were familiar. They also learned the patterning of the pairs.

Such demonstrations that babies and children can detect statistical relationships between features or events reveals a powerful mechanism for learning. Statistical learning enables the brain to learn the statistical *structure* of any event or object. Hence the brain will learn the underlying and perhaps hidden relations that are also described as 'natural cause'. Statistical structure is learned in all sensory modalities simultaneously. For example, as the child learns about birds, the child will learn that light body weight, having feathers, having wings, having a beak, singing, and flying, all go together. Each bird that the child sees may be different, but each bird will share the features of flying, having feathers, having wings, and so on. Hence each unique experience will activate the brain cells that detect flying motion, that detect feather-like texture, that detect singing, and so on. The connections that form between the different brain cells that are activated by hearing, seeing, and feeling birds will be repeatedly strengthened for these shared features, thereby creating a *multi-modal neural network* for that particular concept. The development of this network will be dependent on everyday experiences, and the networks will be richer if the experiences are more varied. This principle of learning supports the use of multi-modal instruction and active experience in nursery and primary school.

Indeed, brain imaging studies with adults using *functional magnetic resonance imaging* (fMRI—this technique measures blood flow in the brain and hence identifies which brain areas are most active) have shown that all of the sensory systems related to experiencing concepts are activated even by just reading the name of the concept. For example, reading the word 'kick' will activate brain cells in the motor system that are used when we kick our legs, even though we are not moving our legs when we read. So knowledge about concepts is *distributed* across the entire brain. It is not stored separately in a kind of conceptual 'dictionary' or distinct knowledge system. Multi-modal experiences strengthen learning across the whole brain. Accordingly, *multisensory learning* is the most effective kind of learning for young children. If learning environments provide a wide range of multisensory experiences, teachers can capitalize on these natural mechanisms of learning and development.

Chapter 3
Learning language

Language is a critical factor for child development. While babies and toddlers learn a lot about the world from objects, they rarely manipulate objects in total silence. Usually the baby will vocalize and hand objects to adults or to older children. In play situations, adults naturally name objects for infants and usually provide some extra relevant information as well. Babies learn words most quickly when an adult both points to and names a new item. Indeed, babies' brains seem to be primed to learn new words with great rapidity. By the age of 15 months, just hearing a new word *once* is enough for accurate learning. Some studies suggest that 2-year-olds are learning around ten new words every day. This is made possible by the brain's remarkable facility for language.

Infant-directed speech

One reason that babies learn language so readily is that we speak to them in a special way. We use infant-directed speech (IDS) or *Parentese*. As noted in Chapter 1, IDS appears to be biologically pre-programmed into our species, and is used by adults and children alike. IDS has a sort of 'sing-song' intonation that heightens pitch, exaggerates the length of words, and uses extra stress, exaggerating the *rhythmic* or *prosodic* aspects of speech. Indeed, sensitivity to speech rhythm has been argued to be a key precursor to language acquisition. Languages actually differ in their characteristic rhythms. Arabic, for example, sounds different rhythmically to French, which is different again to Russian. Experiments based on sucking show that babies as young as 4 days old can discriminate between French and Russian. They seem to do so on the basis of speech rhythm.

The rhythmic or prosodic exaggeration in IDS has a number of important characteristics that support learning. Firstly, the heightened prosody increases the salience of acoustic cues to where words *begin* and *end*. Although we perceive speech as a sequence of words, it is in fact an unbroken stream of sound. We know which bits of the stream are separate words, because we have learned what the words are. We cannot reliably pick out the words in an unknown foreign language. For example, about 90 per cent of English bisyllabic words for things have a 'strong-weak' (or 'loud-less loud') rhythmic pattern, like BA-by, BOTT-le, and COOK-ie. In IDS, the first syllable in a strong-weak pattern receives extra stress, emphasizing for the baby that the word begins *here*. Babies learn that this strong-weak *stress template* characterizes English bisyllabic words. So they begin expecting that word onsets are cued by stressed syllables. Then, if novel words do not fit this pattern, babies mis-segment them. For example, experiments show that 7-month-olds who hear the sentence 'Her guiTAR is too fancy' assume that 'taris' is a novel word. Ten-month-olds no longer make these mis-segmentation errors.

Another effect of talking in IDS is that it captures attention. Babies like IDS and so they listen to it. Experiments have shown that even newborns prefer IDS over adult-directed speech. Although we also speak more loudly and with exaggerated pitch to people that we assume to be foreign, we do not exaggerate prosody in the same way. Similarly, although we appear to speak to pets in IDS, close analysis of the acoustic characteristics of so-called 'pet-ese' show that it is quite different to IDS. Pet-directed speech does not include the exaggerated prosodic contours found in IDS, and it does not include hyper-articulated vowels. So as well as capturing attention, IDS is emphasizing *key linguistic cues* that help language acquisition.

Finally, IDS marks information that is new. In one study, mothers read a picture book to their babies, and researchers measured which words received the most stress. New words received primary stress on 76 per cent of occasions. When new words were read for the second time, they were again highly stressed on 70 per cent of occasions. When the mothers were reading the same book to another adult, this did not occur. Across cultures, similar effects are found. Mothers and other carers are not aware that they are using IDS to teach babies new information, but they are.

Statistical learning of sound patterns

As well as the prosodic and acoustic clues that support word learning, babies are sensitive to *statistical* clues that tell them which sounds belong together and make words. For example, the sounds 'a', 'n', and 't' are much more likely to occur in the sequence 'ant' than in the sequence 'atn'. Indeed, no English words end in the sequence 'atn', although this sequence of sounds does occur in connected speech (e.g., in the phrase 'at night'). In statistical terms, therefore, sounds like 'n' and 't' are more likely to be next to each other *within* a word. Sounds like 't' and 'n' are more likely to be next to each other when they are in *different* words. Statistical learning occurs in other sensory systems too, and for language it doesn't require much input. For language, after hearing a two-minute sequence of novel syllables, babies as young as 8 months could recognize the sound elements that went together. For example, if they heard a continuous monotone stream like 'bidakupadotigolabubidaku.' they recognized that 'bidaku' had been heard before, but that 'dapiku' had not. Interestingly, statistical learning is even more efficient if the syllable stream is sung to the listener, or if speech rhythm cues support the statistical boundaries, as they do in natural speech. So language-learning babies are sensitive to multiple linguistic cues at once, making for more efficient learning.

Sensitivity to native speech sounds

There are over 6,000 languages in the world, yet babies acquire whichever language (or languages) they are exposed to from birth. How do they know which sounds matter for their native language/s? Most babies are acquiring more than one language from birth (90 per cent of the world's population is multilingual), but that still leaves a lot of languages that are *not* learned. The infant brain seems to cope with the 'learning problem' of which sounds matter by initially being sensitive to *all* the sound elements used by the different world languages. Via acoustic learning during the first year of life, the brain then specializes in the sounds that matter for the particular languages that it is being exposed to.

This is called *categorical perception*. For example, we can think of the category of 'p' sounds, and the category of 'b' sounds. To make these different sounds, we move our articulators like our lips in the same way. The only distinctive cue to whether 'b' or 'p' is being spoken is how much we vibrate our vocal chords and obstruct the air flow through our lips. Although different speakers will vary in how much vibration and obstruction they use to create a 'b' sound, as listeners we *categorically* hear either a 'b' sound or a 'p' sound. A variety of different 'b' sounds are all heard as 'b', and then a slight further change in obstruction is suddenly heard as 'p'. Babies as young as 1 month hear these 'categorical boundaries' in exactly the same places as adults. In fact, many animal species discriminate categorical boundaries. Examples include chinchillas, budgerigars, and crickets. As these animals cannot talk, the brain appears to be responding to physical discontinuities in the stimulus that do not depend on knowing what language is being spoken.

Even so, there is important learning during the first year of life. For example, a language like Hindi has three speech sounds in the physical continuum from 'd' to 't', while English has only two speech sounds ('d' or 't'). Indian and English babies younger than a year can hear all three sounds. However, if the native language does not require this sensitivity, it is lost. Hence English babies older than about a year will no longer distinguish all three sounds. Indian babies will continue to distinguish them. Some sound elements are also visible on the lips. Imagine saying the words 'box' and 'vox'. Your lips are making a different shape, and babies are sensitive to these different shapes. For babies younger than a year of age, visual sensitivity is found for all the distinctions made in different languages. However, this visual sensitivity declines with learning. For example, a language like Spanish does not utilize the 'b'/'v' distinction to change word meaning. Spanish words which are written differently, like VASO and BUENO, both begin with the same sound. Indeed, sometimes two spelling forms are allowed to reflect this, as in CEVICHE and CEBICHE. Accordingly, after around a year of learning Spanish, Spanish babies stop distinguishing 'b' from 'v' on the lips *as well as* acoustically ceasing to make this categorical distinction.

Finally, social interactions with caretakers appear to be very important in determining categorical learning. Babies cannot learn the key sound elements of language from the TV. This was shown in a clever experiment that paired Mandarin Chinese graduate students with American English babies. The students played with toys with the babies, speaking all the time in Chinese. Usually, babies who do not hear Mandarin Chinese lose their sensitivity to Mandarin sound categories that are not used in English. However, as these babies were playing daily with Mandarin Chinese speakers, they retained these contrasts. The play sessions were also filmed, and new babies were then shown the Mandarin Chinese graduate students on TV. The films were taken from the babies' point of view, so that the students appeared to be handing toys to infants from inside the TV, etc. While the babies were fascinated by the videos and were highly attentive, frequently touching the screen, the 'TV babies' did not retain the Mandarin sound categories. So even though the 'TV babies' were exposed to the *same amount* of auditory and visual input, learning did not occur without the live presence of the adult.

What babies say

Babies are active partners in conversations from very early on, even before they can say words. Not all vocalizing is speech-like, and indeed between 0–2 months babies produce quite a lot of grunting-type sounds when communicating. However, they also produce 'comfort' sounds which are vowel-like, with normal speech-like phonation. From around 2–3 months they begin 'gooing', producing sequences of speech-like sounds, followed by so-called 'marginal babbling'. Marginal babbling (approximately 3–6 months) does not involve mature syllables, but babies will produce 'proto-syllables' which include trilling and squealing sounds. From around 7 months onwards, full babbling is found. Now babies produce recognizable syllables in repetitive sequences, such as 'dadadadada' and 'mamamama'. These mature syllables can then function as building blocks for words.

Early vocalization is partly determined by the functioning of the *articulators*, the tongue, larynx, lips, etc. that we move to shape sounds into speech. Indeed, babies learning different languages seem to babble the same sounds in the same order. This sequential order seems to be determined by how easy it is to *make* the different speech sounds. Sounds like 'b' and 'p', and nasal sounds like 'm' and 'n', are easier to produce than fricative sounds like 'f', and therefore sounds like 'b' and 'p' appear first. Babies who are born profoundly deaf also babble. However, babbling in deaf babies has a later onset than in hearing babies (between 11 and 25 months), and the babble does not sound as speech-like as the babble of hearing babies. Interestingly, deaf babies who are in a *signing environment* will babble with their hands. They make unique hand movements, hand movements that are not found in hearing babies. These deaf baby hand movements follow the prosodic structures of natural *sign* languages. Hence deaf babies appear to babble the rudimentary *rhythmic* aspects of sign language. Hearing babies babble the rudimentary rhythmic aspects of spoken language—namely syllables.

Although hearing babies are similar across cultures in terms of which speech sounds are babbled first, the rhythmic structure of their babble is quite different. This was shown in an experiment that recorded vocalizations from babies of 6 months in different cultures. These babies were too young to produce any recognizable words. Nevertheless, when adults listened to the tapes, they could easily distinguish babies from their own culture. For example, French adults could pick French baby babble out of French, Arabic, and Cantonese babbling. In fact, the *frequency* of the sounds that are babbled also varies across cultures. For example, the sounds 'b', 'p', and 'm' are more frequent in French than in English. Accordingly, French babies produce more of these sounds than English babies, even though in both cultures these sounds are babbled early.

Late talkers

There are enormous individual differences in how much language young children produce. This has been shown by experiments based on a measure called the *MacArthur-Bates Communicative Development Inventory*. The original measure was based on the first few hundred words and phrases that were typically acquired by American-English children, such as 'Mummy', 'Daddy', 'bye-bye', and 'all gone'. The Inventory has now been translated into over 20 languages. Parents complete the Inventory, marking how many of the words their children know, and fill it in again at different ages. These studies have shown enormous similarity across languages in the first words acquired by young children. They have also shown considerable cross-cultural similarity in the developmental time-course of comprehension and production. At the same time, they have demonstrated large *individual differences* between children acquiring the same language.

For example, in American English, median vocabulary size (the size that occurs most often) at 16 months is 55 words. By 2 years of age, it is around 225 words. By 30 months, it is 573 words, and by age 6 years, it is over 6,000 words. Nevertheless, some children will still not have produced a single word by the age of 2. Yet half of these 'late talkers' will show completely normal development of language by age 5. The other half of these children will go on to have a specific language impairment or will turn out to have another developmental disorder, such as autism. Unfortunately, research has still not been able to identify the factors that differentiate between these two kinds of late talkers. However, other risk signs for autism are known. These include the absence of behaviours that show an understanding of communicative intent, a construct discussed in Chapter 1. If late talking is combined with being less likely to respond to the sound of your name, avoidance of direct eye gaze and an absence of pointing to engage the attention of others, then the risk that autism is present is higher.

The role of gesture

Babies can also clarify their intended communications by using gestures. Some gestures have almost universal meaning, like waving goodbye. Babies begin using gestures like this quite early on. Between 10 and 18 months of age, gestures become frequent and are used extensively for communication. At least four types of gesture can be identified by the age of 10 months. One type of gesture is intended to guide the carer's behaviour, such as pointing to a desired toy. Another type of gesture conveys emotion and expression, such as shaking the head for 'no'. Some gestures involve objects, such as turning the door handle to indicate that you want to go out, or holding a telephone to your ear. Finally, some gestures are made just to engage in shared meaning making, such as pointing to direct another person's attention to an object of mutual interest. As noted in Chapter 1, this type of gesture (proto-declarative pointing) is especially predictive of language development. After around 18 months, the use of gesture starts declining, as vocalization becomes more and more dominant in communication.

Observing babies and their gestures shows that quite complex meanings can be conveyed by simple actions. For example, in one observational study, Billy wanted to convey to his mother that she should choose the book that they would read together. Billy and his mother had a pile of books in front of them. Billy's mother said 'Billy choose one'. Billy shook his head, and said 'no'. Then he said 'mummy', while placing his mother's hand on the pile of books. This communicated the message that Billy didn't want to choose the book, he wanted his mother to choose the book.

Early word learning and word production

By around 18 months of age, most children are producing words frequently. Indeed, one theory of language development proposed a special 'spurt' in word acquisition at around 18 months. It was argued that children suddenly began producing more and more words for things because they had achieved the insight that words are *names for things*. However, careful longitudinal studies have shown that most children do not experience a sudden 'naming burst' at 18 months. Rather, the first word is understood as early as 4 months of age, at least according to current experimental assessments (it could be earlier). The first word understood by a child is typically their own name.

Across different cultures, there is also considerable similarity regarding the first words that young children *produce*. The MacArthur-Bates Communicative Development Inventory reveals that young children produce words for games and routines ('peek-a-boo!'), words for food and drink ('juice', 'cookie'), animal names and animal sounds ('woof woof'), names for toys, and names for clothing and baby items ('bottle', 'bib'). By around 18 months, most children are entering the two-word stage, when they become able to combine words. By using simple constructions such as 'bee window' and 'pillow me!', toddlers can convey quite complex meanings ('There is a fly on the window'; and 'Hit me with your pillow!'). At this age, children often use a word that they know to refer to many different entities whose names are not yet known. They might use the word 'bee' for insects that are not bees, or the word 'dog' to refer to horses and cows. Experiments have shown that this is not a semantic confusion. Toddlers do not think that horses and cows are a type of dog. Rather, they have limited language capacities, and so they stretch their limited vocabularies to communicate as flexibly as possible.

Again, there is a lot of similarity across cultures at the two-word stage regarding which words are combined. Young children combine words to draw attention to objects ('See doggie!'), to indicate ownership ('My shoe'), to point out properties of objects ('Big doggie'), to indicate plurality ('Two cookie'), and to indicate recurrence ('Other cookie'). They also combine words to indicate disappearance ('Daddy bye-bye'), to indicate negations ('No bath'), to indicate location ('Baby car'), to specify requests ('Have dat'), and to indicate who should act ('Mummy do it'). It is only as children learn grammar that some divergence is found across languages. This is probably because different languages have different grammatical formats for combining words.

Conceptual expectations

One reason that babies learn words so easily is that they have *conceptual expectations* about what people are using words for. That is, they appear to have learned that words are labels for things and for actions. Further, babies appear to expect that words will not just name one particular thing, but *categories* of things. In fact, if we study how adults name objects to young children, it turns out that we most often name at the 'basic level' of category. We use labels like 'car', 'dog', and 'tree'. We rarely name *specific types* of car, dog and tree. We also rarely talk at the 'super-ordinate level' about 'vehicles' and 'animals'. Adults' natural tendency to discuss the world at the 'basic level' has been related theoretically to perceptual similarities between entities in the world. For example, dogs are more similar in appearance to other dogs than to horses, even though both dogs and horses are animals with four legs. Cars are more similar in appearance to other cars than to trucks, even though both cars and trucks are vehicles with wheels. Nevertheless, cars and trucks are more similar to each other than they are to horses. One psychological theory about object categorization argues that these *perceptual* or *appearance-based* similarities are usually correlated with important structural similarities. For example, both dogs and horses have legs because they are animate and can move by themselves. Both cars and trucks have wheels because they are man-made and the wheels allow them to move. According to this view, parental naming practices reinforce the perceptual level at which entities are most similar to each other—the 'basic level'.

Another important expectation is that babies expect adults to be *truthful* namers of things. If a baby was surrounded by adults who were deliberately mislabelling objects, it would be much more difficult to acquire language. After all, a label like 'cat' only means 'animal with whiskers and a tail' because members of our culture have essentially agreed that this sound pattern will name this particular entity. 'We' have a shared belief system that the sound pattern 'cat' is used by all speakers to convey information about cats. Babies learn about these norms. For example, in one experiment, babies aged 16 months were shown photographs of familiar objects like a *shoe* and a *cat* while they sat on their carer's lap. The carer wore a blindfold so as not to inadvertently influence the babies' behaviour. As each photo appeared, it was labelled by the experimenter ('shoe', 'cat'). Occasionally the experimenter deliberately mislabelled the pictures, for example labelling a picture of a shoe 'cat'. Mislabelling led the babies to become distressed.

All the babies tried to correct the experimenter, either producing the correct label themselves, or shaking their head, or pointing to their own shoes. Some even tried to remove their carer's blindfold to get help, and some started crying. This brings us back to the importance of *communicative intent* for language acquisition, discussed in Chapter 1. Labels are not simply labels. They also reflect the *intentional states* of speakers.

Linguistic influences

At the same time as having conceptual expectations about 'word-to-world links', babies are influenced by linguistic usage in their particular environmental context. This was noted already for the basic level of object categorization, but the effects of linguistic influences on conceptual development are much wider than this. Indeed, the effect of the words we use on the way that we think and the way that we perceive the world can be documented for adults as well as for babies (the 'Sapir-Whorf' hypothesis). One popular example comes from Whorf's original work, where he noted that describing a petrol drum as 'empty' led people to consider it as harmless. In fact, the drum still contained flammable vapours, even though no fuel was present. Labelling the drums as empty meant that some people disposed of cigarette butts in them. The subsequent explosions came as a surprise—surely the drum was 'empty'. In a similar way, it has been argued that for babies growing up in different linguistic environments, the conceptual world might be carved up differently by linguistic usage.

One nice example in the language acquisition literature comes from spatial concepts. In a language like English, the word 'in' matches *containment* relations—things are 'in' other things. The English word 'on' matches *support* relations—things are 'on' other things, as in 'the cup is on the table'. The cup is being supported by the table in the horizontal plane. However, the English word 'on' also specifies attachment to a surface in the vertical plane.

The fridge magnet is 'on' the fridge, or the doorbell is 'on' the door. This is different from Spanish, which has one word 'en' to refer to all three types of spatial relationship. It is also different from Dutch, which has a different word for each type of spatial relationship. Some linguists argue that these different words for spatial relations affect children's spatial concepts in these different languages. However, most of the research on linguistic influences uses simpler concepts like colour, and has not considered young learners of the languages studied. Perceiving and remembering colours seems only minimally affected by linguistic labels. Some languages have many words for a colour that has only one label in English. Other languages have a restricted set of colour labels that miss out altogether colours that we name in English. Although some experiments with colour words do show effects on perception and memory for colours, the effects tend to be small and context-dependent. So while linguistic usage must influence children's language development, relevant experiments are difficult to design.

Language as a symbolic system

The fact that labels like 'cat' have no inherent meaning, but acquire meanings because of *cultural norms* regarding their use, means that words are 'symbolic'. They have no intrinsic connection to what they are labelling, but they do have a symbolic connection—they stand for the things to which they refer. Words are thus symbols that encode our experiences and that *stand for* concepts and events in the everyday world. This makes words very powerful for psychological development. Once you know the words, you can manipulate symbols *in your mind* to achieve new understandings. You can teach other people your knowledge using words. The Russian child psychologist Lev Vygotsky called human language a 'sign system', a human cultural development that enabled the symbolic representation of knowledge (see Chapter 7). Vygotsky argued that language was a psychological tool for organizing cognitive behaviour. A human could use these symbolic signs not only to communicate with another human, but to communicate with herself inside her head. Language enables us to think about what we know, to plan and to problem solve, and to change our own understandings. Hence language has a transformative effect on psychological development.

One of the transformative effects occurs because language enables children to reflect on their own understandings. In psychological terms, children can now reflect on their own cognitive processes, exploring their own thoughts. This is called 'metacognition'. However, children can also use language to explore their own emotions, feelings, and behaviour. In psychological terms, they can use language for 'self-regulation'. Being able to talk through an upsetting emotional reaction or a situation where one's behaviour led to unintended consequences helps understanding, and helps to prevent the recurrence of unwanted events. Even very young children will use language to regulate their own behaviour and their emotional responses. Indeed, individual differences in language acquisition are connected in important ways with how well children develop conscious control over their feelings, actions, and behaviour (see Chapter 5).

Grammar

The grammars that characterize different human languages are relatively complicated. Because grammatical constructions are complex, it was believed for a long time that there was something unique about language acquisition. In fact, it was thought (for example, by the linguist Noam Chomsky) that babies were born with a special language acquisition device, or innate *universal grammar*. This special device meant that babies were biologically prepared to acquire grammatical structures, while other species were not. More recently, it has been argued that cultural learning and the general learning processes discussed in Chapter 2 (such as statistical learning and learning by analogy) are sufficient to support the development of grammatical learning. By hearing the unique utterances produced by the speakers around them, babies use their general learning mechanisms to extract the underlying structural conventions for word combination that we call grammar. Hence infants *construct* grammar from their listening experiences, supported by feedback from those around them.

As children begin to combine more and more words together, they test out different grammatical possibilities, occasionally making obvious errors ('We goed to the park'; 'It's very nighty!' [looking out at the dark]). Research suggests that adults correct these errors as part of natural conversation. They do not use direct correction (they do not say 'No, we say *we went* to the park'). In natural conversation with their young children, mothers and fathers will re-frame or *re-formulate* the child's utterance into the correct grammatical format ('That's right, we went to the park yesterday'). Between the ages of 2 and 3 years, more and more abstract constructions appear in children's everyday conversations. Children show increasing awareness of the correct *conventions* regarding word order and syntax in the language/s that they are learning. Children learn grammar through language *use*.

Michael Tomasello, an important theorist in language acquisition, calls their grammatical learning 'pattern-finding'. Children will learn a pattern (like [agent] [verb] [object]) and repeat it over and over ('Daddy cut the grass', 'Mummy did the shopping', 'The big dog chased the cat'). Indeed, observational research has shown that toddlers hear certain grammatical constructions literally hundreds of times a day. Constructions such as 'Look at x', 'Here's x' and 'Are you x?' make up approximately a third of the 5,000–7,000 utterances that (middle class) toddlers hear every day. As children get older, the abstract grammatical patterns that they notice and use get more and more complex ('I know she hit him', 'I think I can do it', 'That's the girl who gave me the bike'). So grammatical learning emerges naturally from extensive *language experience* (of the utterances of others) and from *language use* (the novel utterances of the child, which are re-formulated by conversational partners if they are grammatically incorrect).

Pragmatics

As already noted, understanding communicative intent is essential to language-learning. This is because language is a tool for directing the mental states and attention of others. The social and communicative functions of language, and children's understanding of them, are captured by *pragmatics*. For example, we saw that the first word acquired by most infants is their own name. Recognizing your own name is pragmatically very important if other people are trying to communicate with you and include you in their social group. Other pragmatic aspects of conversation include *taking turns*, and making sure that the other person has *sufficient knowledge* of the events being discussed to follow what you are saying. We are all familiar with speaking to young children on the telephone, and only following part of what they are communicating! This is because young children have not yet learned all these pragmatic aspects of conversation. They frequently fail to adopt the perspective of their conversational partner, or they switch conversational topic without warning. These behaviours break the implicit 'rules' of being in a conversation, and impede communication.

The development of pragmatic understanding involves being able to use language both socially and appropriately. This includes understanding what is 'rude' or 'polite' in a certain social context. It also includes being aware of how *familiar* conversational partners are. For example, we might tell a close friend something that we would not tell a neighbour. Indeed, there are many subtle differences in social status that lead an adult to modify their way of communicating (for example, between boss and employee).

Children need experience to learn about all these aspects of pragmatics, and individual differences in social cognition (see

Chapter 4) play a role in how successful they are. The language used in many social routines is actually quite arbitrary. To learn about pragmatics, children need to go beyond the *literal* meaning of the words and make inferences about communicative intent. A conversation is successful when a child has recognized the type of social situation and applied the appropriate formula. For example, a child may have to say polite things when receiving a gift that she does not actually like. Children with autism, who have difficulties with social cognition and in reading the mental states of others, find learning the pragmatics of conversation particularly difficult. Children with conduct disorders also tend to have an impaired understanding of pragmatics.

Chapter 4
Friendships, families, pretend play, and the imagination

Children's experiences within their families vary widely. Yet these experiences have important consequences for social development, moral development, and psychological understanding. When children have siblings, there are usually developmental *advantages* for social cognition and psychological understanding. Siblings can be both allies and rivals, offering opportunities for experiencing affection, reciprocity, support, and of course conflict. However, children's friendships can deliver many of the same advantages. As single child families increase, children's friendships are likely to prove increasingly important for social development.

One of the most important factors for social and moral development seems to be *conversation* around incidents that arise with siblings or friends. Conversations that reflect on the child's feelings, on the psychological causes of other people's actions, and on moral transgressions are particularly effective. The most highly charged emotional situations that children experience usually involve other children. Children's growing understanding of beliefs, desires, and the intentions of others depends on the discussion of these highly charged situations with their families or other carers. Pretend play is another rich means whereby children come to understand beliefs, desires, and intentions, and pretend play with other children (or with an imaginary friend) is particularly important. These imaginary/pretence experiences are critical for giving children insights into 'mental states'. Understanding the mental states of another person allows the child to predict that person's behaviour on the basis of the person's internal beliefs and desires. This social/cognitive understanding is termed developing a 'theory of mind'. People's actions frequently depend on their *beliefs* rather than on objective facts about the world. Learning about these hidden beliefs is a key aspect of social cognition, and develops quite gradually.

'Mind-mindedness' in the family

Although an understanding of mental states develops continually over the child's first years, individual differences can already be measured in infancy. One critical factor in explaining individual differences is whether parents and other caregivers treat babies as individuals with *minds*. We saw in Chapter 1 that forming a secure attachment to the mother and/or other primary caregivers leads to the development of a positive 'internal working model' of the self. Research has also shown that the mothers of babies who are securely attached are more likely to be 'mind-minded'.

Mind-minded mothers interpret the behaviours of the baby as deriving from mental states. This 'mind-minded' attitude appears to help babies to come to understand mental states and the role of mental states in explaining people's behaviour. Young children who are better at understanding the psychological characteristics of other people (those people's *internal mental states*) are also better at understanding their likely behaviour towards the child herself. This means that the child's 'internal working model' of who they are and whether they matter will depend both on the *actual* behaviour of the parent or carer, and also on the *intended* behaviour.

'Mind-mindedness' can be assessed in various ways. For example, babies make a lot of sounds that are not real words, but they may intend these sounds to indicate particular meanings. Mothers who interpret the meanings of the sounds that their babies make as intended speech acts are assessed as more 'mind-minded'. Similarly, mothers who report that they cannot understand their babies, who they consider to be speaking 'double-Dutch' or 'gobbledegook', are considered less 'mind-minded'. These individual differences in maternal behaviour appear to be consistent. For example, in one study the same mothers were revisited when the child was 3 years old, and were asked to describe their child. More 'mind-minded' mothers would describe their child in terms of her/his emotions, desires, mental life and imagination. Less 'mind-minded' mothers focused on facts like height, weight and hobbies. When the children were aged 5 years, they were tested on false belief tasks that assessed their understanding of mental states. Children who had experienced caretaking that was more 'mind-minded' did better on these mental state tasks.

Developmentally, this range of 'mind-minded' behaviours is distinct from factors that lead to *atypical* pro-social development. Children who go on to develop seriously anti-social behaviour—deliberately starting fights, setting fires, defying teachers, and ignoring social norms—tend to have primary caregivers who interpret the infant's or toddler's behaviours as *deliberately hostile*. This 'hostile attribution bias' on the part of the carer infers hostile intent to apparently provocative acts by their child (e.g., breaking a toy). Such acts may be perceived as neutral by other adults. For the child, learning via social interaction and caretaking experiences that many apparent provocations by others do *not* have hostile intent is an important part of social development. Everyone has the inbuilt tendency to interpret acts with negative outcomes to the self as deliberately hostile, but this is often not the case. For example, when a parent is restraining a toddler or preventing them from achieving a desired goal (e.g., by putting the TV remote control out of reach), this is frustrating, but it is not hostile. Via experience, most young children learn to identify the cues that signal a benign intent on the part of the other—they develop a 'benign attribution bias'. Research suggests that young children whose own behaviour is consistently interpreted as evidencing hostile intent by their caretakers go on to interpret the neutral behaviours of other people as deliberately hostile. It is children who develop a *hostile attribution bias* who are at developmental risk for serious anti-social behaviour.

Family conversations and mental state language

Most children begin using mental state words like 'think' during the second year of life, but again there are large individual differences. Even at the one-word stage, children as young as 20 months will use words to refer to internal states like pain, distress, affection, and tiredness. By the age of around 2 years, children will refer to their own physiological states ('I'm too hot. I'm sweating!'; 'I not hungry now'), to the states of consciousness of others ('Are you awake now?'), and to the emotions of other people ('Don't be mad, Mummy!'; 'You boo-hoo all better?'). They will also refer directly to mental states ('Do you think I can do this?'), to the distinction between pretend and reality ('Those monsters are just pretend—right?'), and to dreams ('I had a dream about a dog'). Finally, early emerging topics of discussion concern moral transgression, permission, and obligation ('Matthew won't let me play!'; 'Was he naughty?'; 'If I'm good, Santa will bring me toys'). Despite individual differences, by around 28 months around 90 per cent of children in one (middle class) sample were producing words referring to pain, distress, fatigue, disgust, love, and moral conformity. They were also producing sentences suggestive of some understanding of psychological causation ('I give a hug. Baby be happy'; 'I'm hurting your feelings, 'cos I was mean to you').

Family conversations about feelings and moral transgressions appear to be crucial for this developing understanding. In one study, discussions about feelings with 3-year-olds were found to be most frequent when the child was *arguing*, either with their sibling or with their mother. However, the same study found no difference in the frequency of discussions about feelings with girls versus boys, or in the frequency with which girls versus boys referred to their own feelings. What appeared to be important for children's development was having the conversations. When the same children were 6 years old, they were tested with video vignettes of emotional scenarios between adults and were asked to identify how the adults were feeling at different points during the interactions. Children who had experienced more family talk about feelings when aged 3 years were significantly better at identifying the mental states of the adults in these vignettes as 6-year-olds. These significant associations did not depend on the overall language abilities of the children, nor on the overall amount of mother–child talk in the different families. Rather, it depended specifically on the *frequency* of family discussions about feelings.

Studies such as this demonstrate that having 'normal' (rather than violent and deeply hostile) arguments and fights with siblings and other children is a necessary part of social development. If these disputes are then discussed in the family, identifying their psychological causes ('He was cross because you took his favourite cup'; 'Baby is happy when you do that') then children can learn about their own and others' emotions and mental states. Taking a pre-emptive approach by discussing the feelings and needs of babies or younger siblings can also be effective. The feelings of rivalry inherent in having a sibling in themselves help to develop psychological insights into another's mind, for example as children seek to improve their ability to annoy or upset their brother or sister.

Discussing the *causes* of disputes appears to be particularly important for developing social understanding. Young children need opportunities to ask questions, argue with explanations, and reflect on why other people behave in the way that they do. This helps not only pro-social development, but also the child's understanding of their own internal mental states, their own feelings, and their own behaviours. The mental states of another person cannot be seen directly, but mental states can be inferred from behaviour. Making these inferences successfully is helped by conversations within the family (or preschool) setting. Similarly, it can be difficult to understand one's own feelings in certain situations. Having conversations about mental states, ideally at the time that a flashpoint is reached, helps children to understand both their own minds, and the minds of others.

Finally, being a parent is an emotionally challenging experience, and how parents deal with their own emotions plays a role in effective parenting. It is an unfortunate fact that in some families, parent–child relationships are quite hostile, and parental control strategies are inconsistent and ineffectual, or rely on harsh discipline. In such families, children are more likely to engage in bullying behaviour or physical aggression against other children once they reach school. For example, in one study children from families in which parents reported using control strategies like hitting, grabbing, and shoving the child were more likely to exhibit behaviours like starting fights, disrupting classroom discipline, and being defiant to the teacher. As family interactions are central to the development of pro-social understanding, families that are characterized by sustained (not occasional) violence and aggression to children, a hostile attribution bias on the part of parents, and punitive child control methods, tend to produce children in whom the development of social understanding is impaired.

Unfortunately, these effects can be exacerbated by having violent siblings and peers. Sibling interactions usually mirror the quality of other family interactions, and so families experiencing negative parent–child interactions and marital discord are frequently also experiencing more hostile sibling relationships. For example, one study of 'hard-to-manage' preschoolers showed that their pretend play in preschool was significantly more likely to involve killing others or inflicting pain (e.g., 4-year-old child brandishing a toy sword, and shouting 'Kill! Kill! Kill me!'—his friend dropped his toy sword and said 'no'). These hard-to-manage children also showed impaired moral awareness and social understanding at age 6. Developmental processes are impaired further when language development is poor and 'executive function' skills, which govern the development of self-regulation, are delayed (see Chapter 5).

Pretend play with carers helps psychological understanding

Pretend play provides an important avenue for understanding mental states. Pretend play can be solitary, or with an adult carer, or with other children. A lot of pretend play with siblings and other children is social play. Children will 'play' at being mummy and daddy, or 'play' at being sisters, or 'play' domestic scenes like cooking a meal, or 'play' going to school. Imagining these situations and gaining some control over what happens in them *via playing* appears to be very important for child development.

Pretend play with mothers and adult carers is different from pretend play with other children, but both are important. Pretend play with adult carers is often object-focused. For example, adult and child may pretend to be on the telephone to each other, but the 'telephone' may be a banana. This kind of pretence enables children to 'decouple' the actual object (the yellow, curved banana) from the symbolized object (the telephone receiver). Pretend play around objects helps children to 'quarantine' the real nature of the objects from their symbolic nature. The child can have two mental representations of the same entity at once.

Although pretending with objects begins by being closely tied to the real nature of the objects (e.g., giving a doll a pretend drink from the child's own cup, or from a toy cup), during the second year of life it becomes more abstract. A curled leaf may become a cup. In psychological terms, pretending enables the creation of 'symbols in thought'. An object has a role in a pretend game not because of what it actually is, but because of what it *symbolizes in that game*. A stick might become a horse—in thought, the stick *is* a horse. In this sense, the emergence of pretend play marks the beginning of a capacity to understand one's own cognitive processes—to understand thoughts as *entities*.

Older 2-year-olds will plan pretend games in advance, and search out the desired props. Young children also imitate the pretend play of their carers. Their pretence is generally more sophisticated when an adult is one of the players. Indeed, Vygotsky argued that adults can play an important role in initiating or extending socio-dramatic play for learning purposes (see Chapter 7). Adults can guide play so that it becomes, in Vygotsky's words, 'a micro-world of active experiencing of social roles and relationships'. In Vygotsky's theory of child development, teacher-guided play is an important mechanism for education, as it can support *cognitive* rather than purely social development.

Another important aspect of pretence is sharing mental states. For example, if a stick has become a horse in the game, this only works because all the players in the game 'agree' that the stick is a horse. Hence pretend play shares with language communicative intentions. The players in the game share the *intention* that the stick symbolizes a horse, just as partners in a conversation share the *intention* that abstract sound patterns (spoken words) symbolize certain meanings. In this way, pretend play fosters the development of a symbolic capacity, which appears to be unique to humans. Rather than operating in the here-and-now with actual objects, the child is operating in an imaginary world with symbolic objects. Symbolic representations are an important aspect of human culture—words, drawings, maps, photos, and so on are all representations of aspects of reality, they are not the objects or settings *themselves*. Understanding symbolic representation has a protracted developmental timecourse, but pretend play is an important early mediator.

Play and pretend play with friends and imaginary friends

In contrast to pretend play with adults, pretend play with siblings and friends is more likely to be social pretence, and can be emotionally highly charged. Further, the players are more likely to be equal actors in the drama. Conversations about feelings are more prevalent in pretend play with siblings and friends than in pretend play with caregivers/teachers. This seems to be helpful for developing an understanding of mental states. Social pretence also enables an understanding of *social norms* and of social situations. For example, Vygotsky commented on two sisters who were 'playing' at being sisters—

> the child in playing tries to be what she thinks a sister should be. In life, the child behaves without thinking that she is her sister's sister. In the game of sisters...both are concerned with displaying their sisterhood...they dress alike, talk alike...as a result of playing, the child comes to understand that sisters possess a different relationship to each other than to other people.

Going to nursery or preschool opens up the opportunity for children to have multiple friendships and to experience pretend play that makes high demands regarding imaginary interaction and co-operation. As children get older less time is spent in actual play, and more and more time is spent in negotiating the plot and each other's roles. Studies of pretend play between 3-year-olds show that pairs of children who engage in more mental state talk while pretending perform better in tasks measuring their understanding of mental states a year later. So more pretending is associated with better 'mind-reading' when children are older. Sharing imaginary worlds, reading the intentions of your friends, and discussing co-operatively how to fit everyone's actions and mental states to the game at hand, has beneficial effects on the development of a 'theory of mind'.

Of course, not every child has siblings or friends who live close enough for daily play. And a surprisingly large percentage of children invent an imaginary companion to supplement their friendships. Studies suggest that between 20 per cent and 50 per cent of preschool children have an imaginary friend. First-born children are those most likely to invent an imaginary friend, and girls are slightly more likely to have imaginary friends than boys are. Most children invent a friend who is the same gender as they are, and some children have more than one imaginary friend. Research shows that children who have imaginary friends are no more shy or anxious than other children, and have as many live friends as children who do not invent imaginary companions. However, those children who do have imaginary friends tend to have richer language skills and tend to be better at constructing narratives than other children. Indeed, creating an imaginary companion requires the child to create a detailed story about the imaginary friend's name and appearance, likes and dislikes, and actions and intentions. Hence many aspects of pretend play with friends are also present in pretend play with an imaginary friend, and appear to play a similar role in promoting pro-social development.

Having friends and playing with them is also important for developing understanding of the *emotions* of others. Individual differences in the ability to read and respond to another's emotions play a key role in children's early friendships. For example, being able to sense when a friend is angry or upset, and knowing what is likely to comfort or amuse them, makes a child a popular friend. Friendships can also introduce various moral issues like cheating, not sharing fairly, or intentionally causing harm to another. Again, learning to negotiate these moral dilemmas and learning to respond appropriately to them has benefits for pro-social development. Longitudinal studies suggest that children with good social understanding, successful communication around transgressions, and high levels of shared co-operative imaginary play find it easier to make new friends when they go to school. As friendships necessarily involve more than one person, how pro-social the child's friends are will also affect the quality of children's friendships. For example, studies suggest that children whose preschool friends are rated by their teachers as more pro-social children are more insightful about the new friends they make when they go to school. Children with more pro-social friends also describe less conflict in these new friendships, and rate themselves as liking their new friends more. The significance of *who* you are friends with for the quality of your later friendships appears to begin in the preschool years.

Pretend play and self-regulation

Pretend play is also important because it usually has *rules*. Children are motivated to stick to these rules because they are part of the game. Hence as Vygotsky recognized, pretend play enables the development of successful self-regulation strategies. Usually, children obey rules because they are compelled to do so by an adult, and the rules go against the child's actual desires. For example, the rule might be 'no chocolate until you have had your dinner'. The child's desire may be for the chocolate and not for the dinner. In pretend play, the rules of the game are invented by the players, and being a participant in the game is the *most* desired state. Hence the child's desire necessitates following the rules of the game. If the game involves chocolate, and the chocolate symbolizes poison in the game, then the child won't eat the chocolate.

Russian psychology has studied these aspects of play more than Western psychology. One lovely example is a group of 6-year-old boys who were playing at being firemen (fire fighters). One boy was the chief, one was the engine driver, the other boys were the firemen. The chief shouts 'fire', they all jump into the toy engine, and the engine driver pretends to drive. They reach the fire and the fire fighters jump out to extinguish the fire. The driver jumps out too, but the other boys tell him to get back into the engine, he has to stay with the engine. So he sits in the engine, controlling his desire to be part of the action.

In another example from Russian studies, children were playing at being sentries. Experimenters measured how long they could stand still. Children aged from 3 to 7 years stood still for a shorter time when they were playing being a sentry standing alone in a room. When their friends were also in the room, monitoring whether the sentry kept still, most children could stand still for much longer. Pretend play hence helps the child to self-regulate their desires and emotions. For infants and young toddlers, play is driven by *things*. Switches demand to be operated, stairs demand to be climbed, doors demand to be opened. As children get older, the world of the imagination takes over. Games become complex, they are planned in advance, props are used. Imaginative pretend play is fundamental to child development.

Pro-social behaviour, morality, and social 'norms'

The agreed 'rules of the game' that may characterize pretend play also help children to develop an understanding of *social norms*. Social norms create a social framework in which we feel obliged to act in certain ways. These ways are ultimately beneficial for society. Social norms govern what is obligatory (e.g., we do not intentionally harm others) and what is permissible (e.g., we should help others, but it is permissible to offer more help to family members than to strangers). Social norms also vary across cultures. Individual differences between children in understanding social norms are another important factor affecting pro-social development.

In pretend play, children can create norms and follow them ('to come into our fort, you have to have a light sabre'). Creating norms in play is thought to help to develop general understanding of *cultural* social norms. Again, understanding the intentions of another and understanding others' emotions appear to underpin developmental differences in children's acquisition of social norms. Children who are anti-social either know about social norms but don't care about them (usually termed psychopathic, these children represent only 1 per cent of the population), or more usually are children who are developing in family contexts that do not facilitate understanding of social norms. Families that do not talk about the intentions and emotions of others and that do not explicitly discuss social norms will create children with *reduced* social understanding. Everyone feels anger at an act that harms the self, and it is normal to feel aggression towards the perpetrator. However, many apparently provocative acts are *neutral* in intent. Families who discuss the emotions and intentions around such acts foster the development of an understanding that many such acts were not intended to provoke and harm—facilitating the development of a *benign attribution bias*.

Alternatively, in some families *mis-perception* of an intention to harm can characterize both adults' perceptions of their own children's behaviour, and children's perceptions of the intentions of others (a *familial* 'hostile attribution bias'). As noted earlier, when key attachment figures do not model benign intent and do not discuss the intentions of others as benign, then the hostile attribution bias that we all feel automatically can become entrenched. Unfortunately, serious anti-social behaviour is highly stable. Consider a boy who is walking down the corridor at school when another boy knocks into him and causes him to drop his books. Bystanding boys laugh. Does the boy interpret this as 'disrespect', a malevolent act that is a provocative threat to his reputation and identity? If so, he will act aggressively. Or does he interpret it as a chance act, benign in terms of intent? If so, he will walk away.

Alternatively, children may be too *impulsive* to abide by social norms in emotionally charged situations. Impulsivity will reduce as self-regulation skills develop. Related reseach suggests that children with anti-social behaviour who display a lack of guilt, the callous use of others for their own gain, and a lack of empathy, are those most likely to show persistent severe and highly aggressive patterns of anti-social behaviour. Not all children with a hostile attributional style become chronically aggressive, however. Such children are also at greater risk for depression and anxiety disorders. Studies on effective interventions for such children are currently limited. However, interventions that tackle the origins of a hostile attribution bias, for example by teaching mothers that infants are not capable of behaving with hostile intent, show some promise. Interventions that teach parents methods of using positive rewards to encourage pro-social behaviour rather than harsh discipline may also be successful.

Difficulty in understanding social norms can also accompany some developmental disorders, such as autism. Children with autism often show profound delays in social understanding and do not 'get' many social norms. These children may behave quite inappropriately in social settings (e.g., commenting loudly on how ugly someone is, or showing their distress when given an unappealing gift). Children with autism may also show very delayed understanding of emotions and of intentions. However, this does not make them *anti-social*, rather it makes them relatively ineffective at being pro-social. Children with autism are no more likely than other children to behave aggressively or to be mean to other children.

Ingroup loyalty

Socio-moral principles like reciprocity and fairness are most likely to be modelled within the family, where they bring benefit to all family members. Indeed, young children develop a sense of who is and is not in their 'ingroup' from a surprisingly young age. The 'ingroup' usually extends beyond the family to other 'people like us'. And children, like adults, are more likely to act in pro-social ways to ingroup members. For example, children are more likely to share objects or foods, or to point out useful information, to ingroup members. A large literature in social science demonstrates the crucial role of ingroup members in our everyday lives. Indeed, some evolutionary analyses suggest that sharing with one's group was originally vital for survival. For example, collaboration in hunting was essential for the group to eat. In large-scale societies such as modern Western societies, where our dependence on each other is less obvious, we need *heuristics* or simple mechanisms for co-operating with relative strangers while excluding 'cheaters' or 'free-loaders'. Social evaluation of who is a member of the ingroup is one such heuristic, and is present at a surprisingly young age.

One nice example comes from an experiment using language. Infants aged 10 months from Paris and Boston were studied. The infants were shown identical videos, in which two women were talking, one speaking French and one English. Each woman then offered the infant an identical toy. As they extended the toy towards the infant, it disappeared from the camera shot and two real copies of the toy appeared on the table in front of the infant. The infants in Paris were significantly more likely to pick up the toy offered by the French-speaking woman, while the infants in Boston were significantly more likely to pick up the toy offered by the English-speaking woman. When the paradigm was extended to examine race, and the infants in Boston were offered toys by two English-speaking women, one black and one white, the (white) infants showed no preference between them. This implies that speech community confers ingroup status for infants, while colour does not.

Pro-social obligation to the group also means that we should help ingroup members more, or give them more resources if resources are limited. Even very young children seem aware of these obligations. For example, in a sweet-sharing experiment with dolls, 3-year-olds were given insufficient sweets to distribute, so that they could not give each doll the same number of sweets. The children gave more sweets to dolls who were described as *siblings* and fewer sweets to dolls who were described as *strangers*. When there were sufficient resources, the 3-year-olds shared fairly between all the dolls. In similar experiments with 5-year-old children who were randomly assigned to a 'red t-shirt' group and a 'blue t-shirt' group, the children shared more resources with 'their' group when shown unfamiliar children wearing either red or blue t-shirts in a video, even though group status was completely arbitrary. This suggests an implicit awareness of social attitudes to the 'ingroup' by age 5. Girls were also found to preferentially allocate resources to other girls, whereas boys did not show a gender bias. 'Ingroups' provide a way of organizing social interactions to promote ingroup 'favouritism'. Social learning of cultural 'ingroups' appears to develop early in children as part of general socio-moral development.

Reciprocity and popularity

One reason that children allocate more resources to ingroup members is thought to be an expectation of *reciprocity*. Usually, you can expect reciprocal treatment from your ingroup members—if the situation were to be reversed, they should usually allocate greater resources to you than to an 'outgroup' member. Again, from an evolutionary perspective, such reciprocity was vital for survival, for example in collaborative foraging. Being part of a group is also socially motivating, as it acts to reinforce a child's social identity. Further, being loyal to one's 'ingroup' is likely to make the child more popular with the other members of that group. Being in a group thus requires the development of knowledge about how to be loyal, about conforming to pressure and about showing ingroup bias. For example, children may need to make fine judgements about who is more popular within the group, so that they can favour friends who are more likely to be popular with the rest of the group.

Perhaps unsurprisingly, rapid development in these abilities appears to occur once children enter school. Making accurate judgements is also supported by cognitive skills like multiple perspective-taking ability. However, even children as young as 6 years will show more positive responding to the transgression of social rules by ingroup members compared to outgroup members, particularly if they have relatively well-developed understanding of emotions and intentions. Some researchers have suggested that children with better social understanding are more likely to act as part of a 'gang', approving or even joining in with the misdemeanours of others in their social group. Children's awareness of ingroup and outgroup distinctions can also be shown via studying their understanding of cultural examples of ingroups, such as being a fan of a particular football team. Again, it is children with good social perspective-taking skills (i.e., able to appreciate the psychological perspectives of other people) who show more advanced ingroup/outgroup understanding, as well as children who are members of more social groups (such as after-school clubs, sports clubs, and choirs).

Chapter 5
Learning and remembering, reading and number

Going to school makes dramatic new demands on young children. Rather than occurring as part of everyday experience, learning, reasoning, and remembering become active goals in their own right. Successful school performance requires children to develop knowledge about their own information-processing skills: 'How good is my memory?' Children also need to be able to monitor their own cognitive performance. School requires children to develop knowledge about the kinds of *cognitive* demands made by different classroom tasks. Psychological research shows rapid development in all of these 'meta-cognitive' skills between the ages of 3 and 7 years. Research on children's developing knowledge of their own cognition (*meta*-cognition) is covered here and in Chapter 6. At the same time, young children are dealing with the non-trivial requirements of learning to read and write, and learning mathematics. As both reading and mathematics are cultural inventions that have been developed over hundreds of years, it is perhaps unsurprising that children take a while to acquire them successfully.

Successful remembering

Children develop various kinds of memory, and all are important for learning in school. The types of memory researched by psychologists include semantic memory (our generic, factual knowledge about the world), episodic memory (our ability consciously to retrieve autobiographical happenings from the past), and implicit or procedural memory (such as habits and skills). Memories that can be brought consciously and deliberately to mind (semantic and episodic memory) are clearly required to benefit from schooling, yet implicit memories, habits and skills can also be important. For example, children aged 3–5 years who are shown 100 different pictures once, one after the other, can recognize 98 per cent of them in a recall task ('did you see this one?'). Such experiments suggest that *implicit* recognition memory (visual recognition memory) is well-developed even in very young children. Memory research has also shown that, contrary to popular belief, young children seldom *invent* memories of events that have not occurred. In fact, even very young children can remember distinct (typically unusual or emotionally important) events with great clarity. In one longitudinal study, a 4-year-old recalled that, when he was 2-and-a-half years old, 'I fed my fish too much food and then it died and my mum dumped him in the toilet'. Another child, who was lactose-intolerant, remembered that at 2-and-a-half 'Mummy gave me Jonathan's milk and I threw up'.

When children are very young, they are focused on learning what psychologists term 'scripts' for routine events. Scripts contain knowledge about the *temporal* and *causal* sequence of events in very specific contexts. Examples include 'doing the shopping', 'doing laundry', 'getting ready to go out', and 'eating lunch'. Scripts are important for organizing the experiences and events of everyday life into a predictable framework. These scripts can then be recalled explicitly on demand. Such scripts, or 'general event representations' develop from an early age and their retention is supported when children have regular routines. Regular routines in effect provide multiple learning experiences for understanding everyday life. Developing basic frameworks for storing, recalling, and interpreting particular experiences is fundamental to how our memory systems work, and this is true for adults as well as for children. Scripts are essentially the way in which we structure and represent our memories of reality.

Scripts enable the world to be a secure and relatively predictable place. Knowing what is routine also enables better memory for what is *novel*. Novel events can be tagged in memory as departures from the expected script. An event like having pudding before the main course at dinner time, because the cooking was taking a long time and everyone was hungry, is very memorable because of its rarity.

At the same time, the ways in which parents (and teachers) interact with children has an influence on the development of autobiographical episodic memories. Shared past events that are frequently refreshed via family recollection or discussion in class are (unsurprisingly) retained better than past events that are not refreshed. At the same time, the ways in which children are questioned about past events has an important effect on how much they remember. The use of a series of specific questions ('Where did we go? Who did we see? Who else was with us?') is one effective way of consolidating children's memories. This is particularly true if the adult then *elaborates* upon the information provided by the child. In one research study, mothers were asked to recall a particular event with their 4-year-old child, such as a visit to the zoo. Mothers who asked the same question repeatedly, without elaboration ('What kinds of animals did you see? And what else? And what else?') were less effective in helping their child to store memories than mothers who elaborated their child's information and evaluated it ('Yes, and what was the lion's cage like? Do you remember if we saw tigers?').

When the children were asked to recall these events again when they were aged 5 and 6 years, it was the children with more elaborative mothers who showed better recall. Such children remembered significantly more accurate information. One reason this occurs is because children (and adults) *construct* episodic memories. Episodic memories are stored partly via rehearsing and recalling an experience (as when adults gossip!). Helping children to recall their experiences in an elaborative way aids the construction process. Therefore, prior knowledge and personal interpretation affect what is remembered. The language skills of the child herself are also important. Good language skills improve memory, because children with better language skills are able to construct narratively coherent and extended, temporally organized representations of experienced events.

Finally, talking about the past with one's parents, family, and school friends enables the construction of a personal *autobiographic history*. This is important for developing a sense of self. Younger children use discussion about the past to strengthen their understanding of their family and of their role within the family. School-aged children talk about their autobiographical past to deepen their relationships with their peers. By discussing our past, we are 'sharing ourselves' with others, and cementing our personal relationships. Creating a shared past also makes us members of a community or a social group. Researchers believe that *shared reminiscing* of this nature helps children to learn how to be a 'self' in their particular culture and social group. Aspects of self-definition vary across cultures, with the 'self-story' of the individual assigned more importance in Western societies than in Asian cultures for example.

Learning to learn and to reason

Research with babies and toddlers (see Chapter 2) has already shown us that much early learning is automatic and depends in part on the way that our sensory systems, like seeing and hearing, operate. Human perceptual systems learn information in a way that enables *explanatory frameworks* to develop. For example, the explanatory system for naive physics is organized around a core framework for describing the possible behaviour of cohesive, solid, three dimensional objects. Observation of the dynamic spatial and temporal behaviour of objects, people and animals generates an important evidence base. At the same time, children have brains that are tracking all kinds of statistical co-dependencies. This statistical database is an extra source of evidence to dynamic spatio-temporal relations. In addition, young children seek hidden features to help them to understand what makes objects and events similar. Children seek such features because they are actively learning 'causal explanatory frameworks' for interpreting the world around them. These kinds of perceptual and causal learning are extended by the child's experiences in school.

In addition to inferring *implicitly* the causal structure of events, once at school children also need to make *explicit* these learning processes. Children need to use their learning abilities deliberately. They need to explicitly co-ordinate evidence with theories about how things work. They need to learn how to formulate and test hypotheses deliberately rather than intuitively. This can be achieved via systematic interventions and manipulations. Action—the child doing something active by themselves in a learning situation—appears crucial to causal learning. These processes of learning and reasoning, along with learning by imitation and learning by analogy, must become explicit to optimize development. For example, psychology research shows that as the child becomes able to manipulate different causes and observe the effects of these manipulations, further learning occurs.

In one experiment on causal learning, children aged between 2 and 5 years were given a novel toy machine and told that it was a 'blicket detector'. The children were told that certain objects ('blickets') could be placed on the machine to make it go (the machine lit up and played music). As the children watched, one building block (A) was put on the machine by the experimenter. Nothing happened. Then a second block (B) was added, and the machine began to play music. The children were asked 'Can you make it stop?' Most of them removed just block B—and the machine stopped.

At the same time, the kind of intuitive physical reasoning that was discussed in Chapter 2 can be susceptible to *biases*, exactly because of the operation of our sensory systems. One example is the 'gravity error' found in young children. Young children assume that if an object is dropped, it will fall straight down. Their prior experience of gravity means that this assumption is usually correct. However, when children see a ball being dropped into an apparatus consisting of three opaque twisted tubes which form a visuo-spatial maze, the gravity rule may not apply. Nevertheless, young children seek the ball using a 'straight down' rule. The children apparently ignore the fact that the twisting means that the tube's exit is not directly below its entrance, even though they can observe the twisting. They still apply the gravity rule. So they search in the wrong place.

In fact, adults also make gravity-like errors in more complex situations. For example, most adults still hold an intuitive theory that objects that are dropped fall straight down. Therefore, they think that if a ball is dropped from the window of a moving train, it will fall downwards in a straight line. But in fact the ball doesn't fall straight down, it falls forwards in an arc. This is because the moving train imparts a *force* to the ball, which affects its trajectory as it falls (this is Newtonian physics). Most children (and many adults) employ a *pre-Newtonian* theory of projectile motion, and reason that the impetus imparted by *dropping* governs the fall. For adults and children to reason correctly, using Newtonian physics, direct teaching is required. In fact, brain imaging work suggests that even when we successfully learn particular scientific concepts, such as the Newtonian theory of motion, these concepts do not *replace* our misleading naive theories. Rather, the brain appears to maintain *both* theories. Selection of the correct basis for reasoning in a given situation then depends on effective (and unconscious) inhibition of the wrong physical model.

Inductive and deductive reasoning

Both inductive and deductive reasoning are used by preschoolers, and both types of reasoning continue to be important during schooling. Inductive inferences are ubiquitous in human reasoning. They involve 'going beyond the information given'. A typical inductive reasoning problem might take the form 'Humans have spleens. Dogs have spleens. Do rabbits have spleens?' As all the animals listed are mammals, children as young as 4 years will reason by analogy that rabbits probably do have spleens. However, if children are given the problem in the form 'Dogs have spleens. Bees have spleens. Do humans have spleens?', then they are more reluctant to draw an inductive inference (and so are adults). This is because the most important constraint on inductive reasoning is *similarity* between the premise and conclusion categories. Dogs and bees are not that similar. Successful inductive reasoning also depends on the *sample size*, and the *typicality* of the property being projected.

The most familiar form of inductive reasoning is probably reasoning by analogy. When we use analogies, we are reasoning that two entities are similar not because of their perceptual appearance, but because of a similarity in underlying *structure*. Structural similarity can be simple, as in the analogy that led to the invention of Velcro. Noticing from observation that plant burrs that stick to our clothing have tiny hooks that make them stick, the inventor of Velcro created a material with many tiny hooks. This enabled Velcro to stick by an analogous hooking mechanism. Structural similarity can also be quite abstract, such as the analogy based on the solar system that is used to teach children about atomic structure. This analogy depends on the structural relation of *orbiting*. In the solar system, the planets orbit the sun, while in the atom, electrons orbit the nucleus. In both cases, the orbiting objects hold their paths because of gravitational force.

Although perceptually similar analogies are easier to spot, once children understand the relations or structural similarities in an analogy, inductive reasoning is difficult to impede. For example, research studies with toddlers and 3-year-olds have shown analogical reasoning in a range of different situations. If all the relations in an analogy are understood, then developmental differences in performance will depend on other factors, such as the efficiency of 'working memory'. However, if children do not understand or do not know the relational basis for an analogy, then analogical reasoning will be difficult, even for older children. The same is true for adults. The analogy items in IQ tests are difficult not because they require reasoning by analogy, but because the premises are unfamiliar. For example, it is difficult to complete the analogy '*inches are to length as lumen is to?*' if you do not know that *lumens* are a unit for measuring brightness.

In contrast to inductive reasoning problems, deductive reasoning problems have only one logically valid answer. Deductive reasoning is important for many subjects in school, especially mathematics. Psychology studies measure the development of deductive reasoning via the 'logical syllogism'. In a syllogism, even answers that run counter to known facts may be deductively valid. For example, given the premises:

All cats bark
Rex is a cat

the logically correct answer to the question 'Does Rex bark?' is 'yes'.

In such 'counter-factual' syllogisms, the premises go against our real-world knowledge that dogs bark, and cats meow. However, the plausibility or real-world accuracy of the premises is not the point. The test of reasoning is to make the correct logical deduction, accepting the validity of the premises.

Research shows that even 4-year-old children can solve logical syllogisms accurately, even if they are counterfactual (as in barking cats). However, syllogisms based on familiar premises are easier, at all ages. Experiments have also explored ways to make counter-factual reasoning easier for children. For example, presenting counter-factual premises in play situations (pretending to be on a planet where cats bark) helps young children to reason logically. However, 4-year-olds can also succeed in reasoning about counterfactuals if they are explicitly asked to *think* about the premises. When told:

> All ladybirds have stripes on their backs.
> Daisy is a ladybird.
> Is Daisy spotty?

One 4-year-old commented, 'All ladybirds have stripes on their back. But they don't', and then deduced that Daisy was stripey and not spotty. Hence even young children can recognize that the premises, whatever they may be, *logically imply* the conclusions. As they get older, children become better at reasoning deductively in a range of situations, as discussed in the next chapter. However, the ability to make logical deductions on the basis of premises is clearly available to preschoolers, and children's logical reasoning skills can be recruited to help them to learn by effective primary school teaching.

Learning to read and write

The cultural invention of writing has had a profound effect on human cognition. Printed symbol systems like the alphabet or Chinese characters are visual codes for symbolizing spoken language. Reading is thus the cognitive process of understanding speech when it is represented by a visual symbol system. Put simply, reading is understanding speech when it is written down.

Via writing information down, we can communicate with people not yet born, and we can keep a record of the past. Once we have learned to read, we can also read to change our own brains. For example, we can acquire new information from reading rather than from direct experience. Research studies show clearly that reading is not simply a visual skill, rather it is a *linguistic* skill. Different aspects of linguistic development, such as morphological and semantic knowledge, all play a role in how efficiently a child learns to read. However, the most important aspect of linguistic knowledge for reading acquisition is *phonological knowledge*. This is knowledge about the sounds and combinations of sounds that comprise words in the child's native language. Knowledge about prosodic structures, about word boundaries, and about syllable stress patterns are all important. When we learn to speak, we are not consciously aware of the sound elements that comprise different words. Hence when we learn to read and write, we need to make this phonological knowledge *explicit*. The term 'phonological awareness' has been coined by psychologists to refer to children's explicit phonological knowledge.

Phonological awareness tasks measure children's ability to reflect deliberately on the sound structure of words. For example, children's ability to detect rhyming patterns or stress patterns in words is measured, or to detect and manipulate the individual sound elements in words that we represent by letters. Thus pre-reading children might be asked to detect the word that does not rhyme out of the spoken words 'cat', 'hat', and 'fit', or whether 'pig' and 'pin' begin with the same sound. Individual differences in these kinds of tasks are strong predictors of how quickly and how well a child will learn to read and to spell. The relationship between phonological awareness and reading development is found in all of the world's languages, not just in languages that use the alphabet.

One of the best ways of developing 'phonological awareness' in young children is via the motivation to write. In order to spell a word, we need to think about the sound elements in the word and the sequence in which they occur. Early spellings produced by pre-readers may not be accurate. Nevertheless, if these early or 'invented spellings' show phonological insight, this is a good sign developmentally. A pre-reading child who writes 'B cwyit!' for 'Be quiet!', or 'Hoo lics hane!' for 'Who likes honey?' is showing *good* phonological awareness. Young spellers may also confuse letter names with letter sounds when writing, as in 'HN' for 'hen' (the name of the letter N is being used), or 'My dadaay wrx hir' for 'My daddy works here' (the name of the letter X is used quite ingeniously in this example).

Phonological awareness skills in pre-readers can be enhanced by learning nursery rhymes and by games of word play, including playground chanting and clapping games. Phonological awareness can also be enhanced by musical activities with a focus on syllable 'beats' (e.g., playing a drum to the syllable patterns in a nursery rhyme like 'Pat-a-cake', or marching to the syllable beats in 'The Grand Old Duke of York'). Phonological awareness is also enhanced by singing and other rhythmic co-ordination of voice and an external beat (e.g., rapping). Any games that focus on listening skills, like 'I Spy', are also useful. Activities that enhance children's ability to hear metrical stress patterns (nursery rhymes are often perfect metrical poems), to hear the syllable structure of words, and to hear rhyme, will all support early alphabetic learning.

Given a strong oral language phonological foundation, and good oral language skills, most children will learn the alphabetic code quite quickly, and will be able to recode simple regularly spelled words to sound during the first year of schooling. Once children begin reading, then letter-sound knowledge and 'phonemic awareness' (the ability to divide words into the single sound elements represented by letters) become the most important predictors of reading development. We saw in Chapter 3 that even babies can respond to phonetic boundaries in the acoustic signal (they can reliably discriminate a 'p' sound from a 'b' sound, for example). However, chinchillas and budgerigars can make similar distinctions. The sound elements represented by alphabetic letters are an *abstraction* from the acoustic signal, and are unlikely to be learned easily by chinchillas or budgies. For example, the words PIT and SPOON both use the letter P to symbolize a 'p' sound, but in the word SPOON the corresponding sound is actually closer to 'b'. Indeed, beginning spellers make mistakes, like writing SBN, *because* they can hear such distinctions. Hence phonemic awareness largely develops as a *consequence* of being taught to read and write. Research shows that illiterate adults do not have phonemic awareness. In fact, brain imaging shows that learning to read 're-maps' phonology in the brain. We begin to hear words as sequences of 'phonemes' only *after* we learn to read.

Dyslexia

Children who are at risk for dyslexia usually struggle with phonological awareness tasks. Impairments are found at all phonological levels (stress pattern, syllable, rhyme, phoneme). This appears to be because some aspects of auditory processing are less efficient in the dyslexic brain. Surprisingly, the auditory cues to the phonetic categories that underpin phonemes seem to be heard well by individuals with dyslexia. In fact, some research suggests that phonetic distinctions may be heard *too* well in dyslexia. Dyslexic children may continue to hear the extra possible divisions of phonetic continua that are discarded by most infants at around 12 months (see Chapter 3). Recent research also suggests that children with dyslexia have difficulty in hearing *prosodic* acoustic cues, for example the acoustic cues to *syllable stress* and *speech rhythm*. These acoustic difficulties are also found in children learning to speak languages like Chinese, which are not written alphabetically (hence phonemic knowledge is not required for reading). Chinese characters represent individual syllables. These broader acoustic difficulties with prosodic structure appear to impair the cognitive process of understanding speech when it is written down, irrespective of the visual symbolic code used by a particular language. Rather few written languages include marking of syllable stress (Greek and Spanish are two examples).

On the other hand, these acoustic difficulties may *manifest* differently in different languages. For example, there are big differences between children with dyslexia learning different alphabetic languages, such as Finnish versus English. A crucial factor is the *consistency* with which letters represent sounds (phonemes) in languages. Phonemes have a *variable* representation in English (e.g., cough, rough, through). In contrast, a language like Finnish has a very consistent spelling system. Consequently, Finnish dyslexic readers learn about phonemes slowly but efficiently, and can be very accurate (albeit slow) readers. English dyslexic readers will be both inaccurate and slow.

Nevertheless, dyslexic children in all languages so far studied are poor spellers. This is because most languages offer multiple choices when going from sound to spelling (e.g., the rhyme sound is spelled differently in 'hurt', 'Bert', and 'skirt'). Likewise, Chinese children with dyslexia are slow and effortful readers even though they do not have to develop phonemic knowledge at all. The auditory processing difficulties found in dyslexia do not seem to affect oral communication—dyslexic children speak and understand oral language very well. This is probably because the auditory difficulties in dyslexia are quite subtle, and speech carries many redundant cues to meaning.

Learning about number

The second symbolic system that has had a profound effect on human cognitive development is the number system. Representing the real world and some of its physical relationships (waves, probability, force) in terms of numbers and equations has enabled us to manipulate those relations and design novel technological systems. Many of these novel systems, like the computer and the internet, now enhance cognitive development for a new generation. Just like learning to read, learning about number requires some years before fluency is acquired. Learning about number also requires direct and specialized teaching. Like reading, however, there are some key cognitive pre-requisites which will affect how well and how quickly children can learn numerical relations when they go to school. One of the most important is a good knowledge of the sequence of counting numbers (1, 2, 3, 4 . . .). This is because the count sequence is the symbolic code for magnitude in an ordered scale, just as the alphabet is the symbolic code for spoken language.

The number system not only represents our knowledge about quantities and magnitudes, numbers represent *exact* quantities. While even babies can judge that a visual array of 16 dots is 'more' than a visual array of 8 dots, the number labels 'sixteen' and 'eight' tell us exactly how much more 16 is than 8. Once we have learned the count sequence, we can also decide where to fit a particular quantity in the overall range of possible quantities. We can also deduce that 16 is a larger number than 8, because it comes later in the sequence. By analogy, we can also deduce that 116 is a larger number than 108, and that 16,000 is a larger number than 8,000. We can also decide that '8 pebbles' is the 'same' as '8 giraffes' in magnitude, because in each case there is a set of 8 entities. The magnitude of each set is the same, even though these sets look very different perceptually.

Young children often acquire quite a long section of the count sequence by the age of around 3 years. However, research suggests that this is *not* the same as understanding what these labels mean mathematically. Nevertheless, repeated experience of counting in different contexts helps children to understand the *number principles* represented by counting. These include one-to-one correspondence (in the example above, there is one pebble for each giraffe), and the need to count each object in a set once and once only. Another principle is the need to count in a stable order, using the same oral sequence each time. If you forget a number word or miss it out, you will be wrong about total set size. Children gradually learn about these meanings of number words via practice and experience.

In Chapter 2, we saw that babies have an apparently innate 'sense' about number, based on an appreciation of both small numbers and of overall magnitudes. One psychological theory is that the brain has an 'analogue magnitude representation'. This is an internal continuum for judging quantity, whereby more brain cells are active for larger quantities. This analogue magnitude system is coupled with an internal system for identifying small numbers. The internal magnitude continuum is applied by babies and children (and animals) to all kinds of quantities, including size and weight as well as number, enabling good imprecise judgements about quantities. Although imprecise, these judgements are nevertheless useful for daily action. These judgements are theoretically made on the basis of the analogue magnitude representation. Thus children (and animals) can distinguish large quantities like 20 versus 40. This ability is *ratio-sensitive*. When sets differ by a great amount in their overall proportion (as in 20:40, where the ratio is 1:2, and as far as possible from 1), children and animals do very well in magnitude judgement tasks. When stimuli differ by a smaller amount (as in 20 versus 22, where the ratio is 10:11, i.e., close to 1) children and animals do very poorly in judging magnitude.

At the same time, children (and animals) can be very precise in making judgements about the magnitude of small numbers (essentially, this has been shown for the numbers 1, 2, and 3 only). It is thought that a perceptual system for *object individuation* (a visual ability to distinguish unique objects in the environment) underpins this relative accuracy with small number judgements. An example is the Mickey Mouse doll experiments discussed in

Chapter 2. However, making perceptual alterations to the display can affect the accuracy of this small number system quite dramatically in some circumstances. For example, if displays of 1 or 2 dots are used, and visual factors like the total filled area, the dot image size and item density are controlled, then babies can no longer distinguish 1 from 2.

Nevertheless, currently it is thought that the analogue magnitude system and the object individuation system are the two core brain systems that underpin the human ability to learn a number system. Regarding individual differences in number processing, researchers disagree over whether children with specific difficulties (*dyscalculia*) have an impaired analogue magnitude representation. No current theories of dyscalculia propose an impaired object individuation system Even so, learning about number as a symbolic system requires cultural learning in school. Simplifying somewhat, we can say that just as we can all learn to speak, but not all of us can learn to read rapidly and efficiently, we can all recognize small and large numbers, but we do not all become highly skilled mathematicians.

Successful mathematical learning in school is facilitated when children have a good knowledge of number names and a good knowledge of the sequence in which they should be applied. These children seem to develop intuitive ideas about numbers that reinforce teaching received in school. Therefore, early learning of the count sequence, and experiencing its relationship to real world entities (counting as you go up the stairs, using counting in board games like *Snakes and Ladders*, counting as sweets are shared) provides social and cultural support for the development of a symbolic number system. Learning the 'language of counting' before schooling appears to given children an advantage when they begin to be taught arithmetic and mathematical operations.

Chapter 6
The learning brain

Across cultures, one goal of schooling is to transmit cultural inventions, such as reading, writing, and number. A second goal is to detach the logical abilities that we all possess from our personal knowledge. Personal experience is a very powerful determinant of how we apply logical reasoning in new situations. In fact, if they cannot verify for themselves that simple premises are true, *unschooled* adults will refuse to reason deductively about these premises. If given a deductive reasoning problem with premises like

> In the far north, where there is snow, all bears are white. Novaya Zemlya is in the far north and there is always snow there. What colour are the bears?

peasants who live in the flatlands will refuse to answer. They say that they cannot tell, and that the questioner should ask someone who lives there. Schooling helps children to detach logic from personal knowledge and solve such logical syllogisms. Schooling also helps children to recognize when to suppress their real-world knowledge of whether premises are plausible, so that they can reason on the basis of the information as given.

In essence, schooling helps children to become 'reflective learners'. During schooling, there are dramatic improvements in 'meta-cognitive' skills (awareness of one's own cognition). For example, via schooling older children learn how to overcome the different biases that impede successful reasoning, such as the 'confirmation bias', discussed later. They also learn strategies for maximizing the effectiveness of their memories. Similarly, there is rapid development in 'executive function' skills (self-monitoring and self-regulation). Executive function (EF) skills include gaining strategic control over your own mental processes, and being able to stop or 'inhibit' certain thoughts or actions. As EF skills develop, the child gains conscious control over her thoughts, feelings and behaviour.

At the same time, school provides powerful social learning experiences, not all of them happy ones. Whereas moral development and pro-social development are facilitated by being in school, so are insights into bullying and the effective control of others. Indeed, the social aspects of being at school involve children in emotionally powerful experiences. As well as supporting further socio-moral development, these experiences can be very memorable, and help to develop the 'autobiographical self'.

'Meta-cognitive' knowledge

Meta-cognitive behaviour is *self-reflective learning behaviour* and is very important for success at school. Meta-cognitive knowledge includes the ability to reflect on your own information-processing skills, the ability to monitor your own cognitive performance, and the ability to be aware of the demands made upon you by different kinds of cognitive tasks. Children with stronger meta-cognitive skills have an advantage at school. They can use their meta-cognitive skills to optimize their own learning. For example, they can consciously reflect on and adjust their memory and reasoning strategies.

In general, children are quite good at monitoring themselves as memorizers. For example, children can be aware of their strengths and weaknesses in remembering certain types of information. Some mnemonic strategies, like rehearsing information under one's breath, seem to come in fairly early developmentally. For example, one study compared 5-year-olds' and 7-year-olds' performance in remembering a set of pictures over a short delay. Only 10 per cent of the 5-year-olds spontaneously rehearsed the picture names to themselves during the delay period. In contrast, 60 per cent of the 7-year-olds used rehearsal. Further work has suggested that 5-year-olds are quite capable of using rehearsal, but that they often don't recognize that rehearsal could be helpful. As they get older, children learn that mnemonic strategies like rehearsal will improve their learning, and so they employ them more frequently.

Similar developmental effects are found for other mnemonic strategies. An example is meaning-based association. In one experiment, 4-year-olds and 6-year-olds were compared in a memory game that involved hiding toy figures (doctor, farmer, policeman) in little houses. The game was to retrieve the figures on demand. The houses had little picture signs on the doors, for example a *syringe*, a *tractor*, and a *police car*. The experimenters found that the 6-year-olds were more likely to use the signs to help their memory than the 4-year-olds. The older children would hide the doctor in the house with the syringe, and the policeman in the house with the police car. Again, the problem for the younger children seemed to be *realizing* that an associative strategy might benefit their memory performance. The 4-year-olds could recognize the associations between syringes and doctors, etc., they just didn't use them in the game.

One main feature that determines later memory development is children's growing understanding of how their memory works. Being able to monitor and regulate one's own memory behaviour enhances performance. Children develop knowledge about their own strengths and weaknesses and acquire knowledge about the demands made by different classroom tasks. They also develop knowledge about the different mnemonic strategies that they can use, and knowledge about the contents of their own memories. Further, children get better at *combining* a range of strategies. For example, in one study children aged 4–8 years saw videos of other children trying to remember ten events from their holidays by looking at a photo album. Some children labelled the pictures, others looked at them silently. The children watching had previously experienced the same task themselves. The researchers found that the children who gave mentalistic explanations for strategic behaviour ('it helped get them into my mind') were those most successful at remembering. Developments in memory ability tend to be characterized by *sudden insights* that a certain strategy might be helpful. Once the insight is achieved, children then continue to use a particular strategy, improving their subsequent memory performance.

Self-monitoring of personal success is also important. Researchers have used a range of measures to assess individual differences in self-monitoring by children. Children may be asked to make 'ease of learning' judgements, or to make judgements about their own learning, or to rate their 'feeling of knowing'. In one study, children aged from 6 to 12 years were asked remember both 'easy' and 'difficult' material (the easy material was remembering highly associated items like 'shoe-sock'). Only some children spent more study time on the harder items, and in general these were the older children. Although the younger children could tell the experimenters which items were easy versus difficult, they did not use this 'ease of learning' knowledge to change their strategic behaviour.

Other measures of meta-cognitive ability, like judging how well one has learned something, seem to differ less between younger and older children. In fact, both children and adults tend to be *over-optimistic* about their learning. Both children and adults rate themselves as likely to perform better than turns out to be the case. Younger children are less good at planning their learning behaviour, however. For example, they are less efficient at deciding which strategies fit a particular situation. Younger children also seem to have more difficulty in keeping track of the sources of their memories than older children. Currently, the view in the literature is that self-monitoring is relatively well-developed, even in young children. What develops is the self-regulation skills (EF skills) that enable a child to apply this knowledge to their *own learning behaviour*.

'Executive function' skills

Executive function abilities are processes that enable you to gain strategic control over your own mental processes. Executive functions encompass the ability strategically to inhibit certain thoughts or actions, the ability to develop conscious control over your thoughts, feelings and behaviour, and the ability to respond flexibly to change. All of these skills develop gradually in children, but there is a developmental spurt in executive function in the primary school years. Individual differences in the rate of development of EF skills are associated with general cognitive ability (non-verbal IQ), with language skills, and with 'working memory' skills (covered further later in this chapter).

In young children, EF abilities are typically measured by tasks like the ability to delay the gratification of a desire. For example, a child might have to wait to take a sweet that is visible underneath a glass until an experimenter rings a bell. EF abilities are also measured by 'conflict' tasks. In conflict tasks (referring to mental conflict), the easier (most *salient*) response is the wrong response. For example, the child might have to say 'day' to a picture of the moon, and 'night' to a picture of the sun. These tasks also measure 'inhibitory control'. Inhibitory control is the child's ability to inhibit the *incorrect* response in a particular situation, even if this response is the habitual response. Children with good inhibitory control can deliberately modulate their own emotional responses and can inhibit inappropriate actions. This improves their social experiences as well as their learning abilities.

EF abilities have important developmental links to success in school. For example, the ability to inhibit task-irrelevant information is important for effective classroom learning. Children with attentional disorders find it very difficult to exert inhibitory control. They tend to be impulsive and disruptive in class. Their inability to ignore irrelevant information also has a negative effect on their learning, even when they have high verbal and non-verbal abilities. Children with anti-social behaviour disorders also lack inhibitory control. Their lack of inhibitory control is often exacerbated by poor language skills. Poor language skills make the child less effective at controlling his or her thoughts, emotions, and actions via inner speech.

Another hallmark of EF is cognitive flexibility. Cognitive flexibility involves skills like shifting mentally backwards and forwards between different tasks, and holding multiple perspectives in mind. Holding multiple perspectives in mind also requires good 'working memory'. Planning is another important aspect of EF. For example, efficient planning and efficient inhibitory control must be combined for effective self-control. Experimenters have devised tasks to distinguish between inhibitory control, working memory, attentional flexibility etc., and there is now a large and fractionated literature. However, experiments tend to show that all these aspects of EF are developing *together*.

Performance in EF tasks also correlates highly with performance in the 'mental state' tasks discussed in Chapter 4 ('theory of mind'). This is not surprising. Executive function tasks measure what the child knows about her own mind. Theory of mind tasks measure what the child knows about somebody else's mind. When gender differences are found, girls outperform boys at all ages, possibly because language skills on average tend to be more advanced in girls.

Meta-cognition and executive function in older children

As children get older, they develop increasing strategic control over their own behaviour, and this applies to their *cognitive* behaviour as well as their *social* behaviour. These developments are critical in order to benefit from schooling. In particular, studies show that children with poor inhibitory control suffer both socially and cognitively. Cognitively, strategic control over one's own mental processes supports efficient learning. Older children's ability to inhibit responses to irrelevant stimuli is usually measured while they are pursuing a cognitively represented goal (i.e., something held in mind), and not an immediate reward in the environment (like the 'sweet under a glass' task used with younger children). The 'irrelevant stimuli' in such experiments can be a range of both cognitive and social distractors.

There are all kinds of 'task irrelevant' information that can get in the way of efficient reasoning or efficient social behaviour. For example, real-world knowledge can impair the 'pure' application of reason. This applies to adults as well as to children. Similarly, a child's current desires or emotional states can affect reasoning abilities, and conflicting information (where the choice of what to suppress is not obvious) can make successful solutions more difficult to recognize. For older children, classic 'inhibitory control' tasks include rule-following tasks with rule switches (e.g, sorting a pack of cards on the basis of colour [hearts go with diamonds], and then on the basis of suit [hearts go with clubs]), and tasks involving arbitrary delays, such as not playing on a pinball machine until told to 'go'. Studies using such tasks suggest that individual differences between children in inhibitory control do not depend on age, gender or IQ. Rather, individual differences continue to depend on language development (verbal ability) and the development of 'working memory'. Working memory is important for managing conflicting *mental* representations efficiently—for example, in the card sort task.

More recently, the developmental psychology literature has made a distinction between 'cold' EF, and 'hot' EF. When the tasks used to measure performance are purely cognitive, such as a number learning task, then EF is said to be *cool*. When tasks involve emotional events, or events with emotionally significant consequences, EF is said to be *hot*. It is more difficult to exert inhibitory control in hot situations. Again, this is also true for adults. Decisions and judgements in emotionally significant situations are usually studied by tasks involving gambling, or computer games involving wins and losses. In general, 'hot' and 'cool' EF seem to develop in similar ways, but may be associated with different areas of the brain. In fact, work with adolescents suggests a *relative decline* in the ability to make judgements in more emotionally loaded situations compared to younger children. Recent research suggests that the adolescent brain undergoes considerable re-wiring, which has a temporary depressive effect on EF skills. Also, adolescents are more susceptible to the peer group. Hence for example, 'hot' EF situations of (apparent) social ostracism can produce very poor judgements by adolescents. Adolescents also tend to discount the future (they underestimate the effect that a current choice will have on their future choices).

Working memory

'Working memory' is a working store of information that is held in mind for a brief period of time, in a 'mental workspace' where it can be manipulated. For example, 'verbal working memory' is the capacity to hold information verbally in mind, perhaps while seeking somewhere to write it down. There is also 'visuo-spatial working memory', the ability to hold information in the 'mind's eye'. One form of visuo-spatial working memory is to imagine an image of the information. Working memory is conceptualized as having a 'limited capacity'. Most people can only hold a certain amount of information in mind at a time. They might also lose the information out of working memory if they are distracted or interrupted. Working memory capacity increases with age throughout childhood, and with expertise, plateauing during the teenage years. It also shows large individual differences. Children with poor working memories will struggle to retain instructions, or to know where they are in a set piece of classroom work, frequently losing their place. Having a poor working memory can cause poor academic progress. The developmental causes of poor working memory are currently not well-understood. For example, individual differences in working memory seem unrelated to the quality of social and intellectual learning environments at home.

Verbal working memory has important developmental links to the concept of 'inner speech'. This is the 'voice in our heads' that we *intuitively* feel we are using when we consciously retain information (e.g., a telephone number) or manipulate it (e.g., plan a course of action). Vygotsky argued that an important aspect of language development was the internalization of speech at around the age of 3–4 years. This is when children typically stop commenting aloud on their behaviour. By Vygotsky's account, 'inner speech' then becomes fundamental in organizing the child's cognitive activities and governing the child's behaviour (see Chapter 7).

Improving reasoning skills

The development of both inhibitory control and working memory also has important effects on the development of reasoning abilities. For example, older children are better at complex inductive reasoning tasks such as analogies than younger children. To solve complex analogies, children have to hold a number of premises simultaneously in working memory. They need to integrate the important relations while simultaneously *inhibiting* irrelevant information. Older children perform better than younger children because they have better inhibitory control and better working memories. Indeed, for deductive reasoning, older children can outperform elderly adults. One example is the solution of 'conflict' syllogisms. In conflict syllogisms real-world knowledge and logic are in conflict. An example is 'All mammals can walk. Whales are mammals. Therefore, whales can walk'. A non-conflict syllogism might be 'All mammals can walk. Apes are mammals. Therefore, apes can walk'. The conclusion that 'whales can walk' is an accurate logical deduction given the premises. The fact that whales cannot walk in real life has to be inhibited to reach the correct solution. Research shows that both younger children and elderly adults perform more poorly with these kinds of syllogism than older children. The younger children are poorer at inhibiting their real-world knowledge, and the elderly adults are suffering an age-related decline in inhibitory control.

Of course, irrelevant background knowledge can only be inhibited successfully if it is known in the first place. This means that younger children, who may lack some kinds of background knowledge, may perform *more* successfully in certain deductive reasoning tasks. Six-year-olds indeed outperform adults in statistical 'base rate' problems, where social stereotype information tends to impede reasoning ability. In one experiment, participants were told that a sample of 30 girls contained 10 girls trying to be cheerleaders, and 20 girls trying out for the school band. They were then asked whether a 'popular and pretty girl who loved people' was more likely to be trying out as a cheerleader or a band member. The correct answer (a band member) was given significantly more often by the children compared to the adults. The 6-year-olds lacked social stereotype knowledge about cheerleaders, and so it did not affect their probability judgements.

From novice to expert

In general, schooling is a time when children move from being *novices*, with little knowledge of the world beyond their personal experience, to relative *experts*. Acquiring more knowledge is the developmental driver of expertise. Indeed, experts organize their memories in different ways to novices. Experiments with child prodigies, for example in chess, demonstrate that expertise does not simply accompany age. The young chess master has played many games already, and her accumulated knowledge about chess enables her to out-play grown-ups. Experiments on expertise show that depth of prior knowledge has a significant effect on how *new information* is encoded and stored. Expertise also improves the efficiency of recall. Indeed, studies of child 'soccer experts' suggest that having knowledge—lots of expertise—is more important than general cognitive ability for memory performance. So the saying 'practice makes perfect' captures something important about how knowledge develops.

Scientific reasoning and hypothesis-testing

Scientific reasoning has traditionally been assumed too difficult for young children. Yet children as young as 6 years of age are able to understand the goal of *testing a hypothesis*. They can also distinguish between conclusive and inconclusive tests of that hypothesis in simplified circumstances. For example, in one experiment children aged 6 and 8 years were told a story about two brothers who thought that they had a mouse living in their house. One brother believed this mouse was a 'big daddy mouse'. The other brother believed it was a 'little baby mouse'. To test their theory, the brothers were planning to leave a box baited with cheese out at night. The children were shown two boxes, one with a large opening, and one with a small opening. They were asked which box the brothers should use to decide who was right. The majority of the children reasoned that the brothers should use the box with the *small* opening. If the cheese was gone the next day, then the mouse was small. If it was still there, then the mouse must be big.

Children (and adults) find hypothesis-testing more difficult when there are multiple competing causal variables in a situation. Hypothesis-testing is also more difficult when pre-existing knowledge gets in the way of designing a pure test. While children's basic causal intuitions are usually sound, the need to co-ordinate multiple kinds of evidence to differentiate between different theories develops relatively slowly. For example, in one study children aged 11 and 14 years were unable to identify which kinds of food at a particular boarding school were causing some of the children at the school to get colds. As causal evidence, the 11- and 14-year-old participants were shown pictures of foods (like apples, chipped potatoes, Granola, and coca-cola). These foods co-varied systematically with whether children at the school (shown in pictures next to the foods) had colds. Despite the systematic co-variance information, only 30 per cent of the 11-year-olds and 50 per cent of the 14-year-olds could identify the critical foods. Many of the errors involved attributing a causal role to a food that only co-varied with a child having a cold on a single occasion ('inclusion errors').

Part of the reason for these systematic inclusion errors appeared to be pre-existing causal knowledge. In the foods study, children may have had strong prior beliefs about which kinds of foods were healthy. This prior knowledge may have interfered with identifying the foods that systematically co-varied with getting a cold (one of which was apples, usually considered healthy, see Figure 7). There is also a strong 'confirmation bias' in human reasoning, found at all ages—we tend to seek out causal evidence that is *consistent with our prior beliefs*. This is a major source of inferential error in fields as disparate as science, economics, and the law, as well as in classroom scientific reasoning.

Like memory skills, reasoning skills also improve as children become aware of how their reasoning processes work and can reflect on them strategically. For example, learning that there might be multiple causal factors determining a particular outcome enables children to devise better ways of testing hypotheses. Most causal reasoning situations in real life are multidimensional, and so are most scientific problems. In order to identify likely

Child Psychology

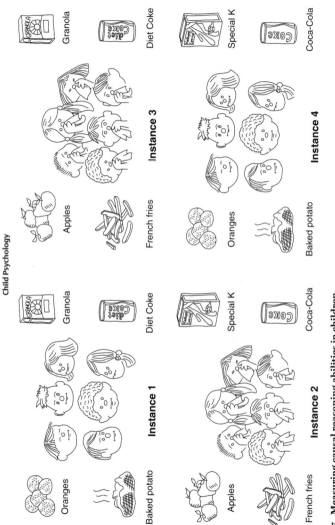

Oranges
Baked potato

Instance 1

Granola
Diet Coke

Apples
French fries

Instance 3

Granola
Diet Coke

Apples
French fries

Instance 2

Special K
Coca-Cola

Oranges
Baked potato

Instance 4

Special K
Coca-Cola

7. Measuring causal reasoning abilities in children

outcomes, we cannot reason about causes and effects in isolation of each other. As children get older, they get better at inter-relating different causal dimensions, and in handling more dimensions. This is partly governed by increased capacity in working memory. Children also get better at overcoming the 'confirmation bias'.

Further, *direct teaching* of scientific reasoning skills helps children to reason logically independently of their pre-existing beliefs. This is more difficult than it sounds, as pre-existing beliefs exert strong effects. Of course, in many social situations we are advantaged if we reason on the basis of our pre-existing beliefs. This is one reason that stereotypes form, which as we have seen play a key role in socio-moral reasoning (e.g., via 'ingroups' and 'outgroups', see Chapter 4).

Extending moral development

The powerful opportunities for social learning offered by communities like schools means that important changes in moral reasoning also occur during the later years of schooling. We saw in Chapter 4 that even very young children can differentiate between morality (not deliberately inflicting harm or injustice) and social convention (context-dependent rules, such as wearing school uniform). At the same time, younger children find it difficult to make moral judgements when they have to keep conflicting information in mind. An example might be when the needs of more than one person are at stake. As growing EF, working memory, and meta-cognitive abilities enhance the child's capacity to handle complexity, children's moral thinking becomes more nuanced and complex.

One interesting example is 'bystander behaviour'. For example, one set of experiments explored children's moral intuitions about what they should do if they saw someone unwittingly drop some money. Younger children studied (8-year-olds) thought that keeping the money for oneself was wrong. Thirteen-year-olds were quite likely to argue that they should be allowed to keep the money. In contrast, 16-year-olds agreed with the 8-year-olds that keeping the money oneself was wrong. Questioning revealed that the 13-year-olds reasoned that the money would be lost to the owner even if the owner had not observed its loss, and therefore it was okay to keep it. The 16-year-olds recognized that the very act of observing its loss obligated them to return the money to its owner. The 8-year-olds simply reasoned that the money was the property of its owner, and therefore should be returned. Interestingly, all the age groups studied were *equally* likely to return the money when told that the person dropping it was disabled.

Social conventions vary with culture, and children's reasoning about social conventions in their own culture reflects their growing understanding of social organization and its underlying social drivers. Whereas younger children (10-year-olds) assume that people in charge make up the rules, adolescents recognize that the rules per se are arbitrary. However, while younger adolescents (13-year-olds) conceptualize social rules as the dictates of authority, older adolescents (16 years and older) understand that social conventions have meaning within a broader social framework. Social conventions are seen as upholding a *social system* of fixed roles and obligations. Again, there are cultural variations, with children growing up in more traditional cultures being less likely to view social conventions as open to change. As with logical reasoning, however, a primary factor in development is the ability to *reflect* on one's knowledge and understanding to gain deeper insights.

For some aspects of social convention, this reflection leads to the recognition of inconsistencies. For example, social conventions about gender norms (which vary widely across cultures) may conflict with moral concerns about what is fair or just. There is also some research suggesting that females are more likely to develop a 'morality of care', in which people's needs are prioritized.

Males are more likely to develop a 'morality of justice', based on fairness. Large meta-analyses suggest, however, that the genders are far more similar than different in their moral development.

It has also been argued that children's *own experiences* essentially provide the raw data for moral reflection. For example, the emotional experience of being the target of an undeserved physical attack, a target of theft, or a target of name-calling, might yield an understanding of what it means to be unfairly victimized. Deeper understanding is also in some sense a double-edged sword, as it can increase children's sensitivity to the hurtful comments or behaviours of others. Deeper understanding may even help some children to become more effective bullies. Such children will use their understanding of group dynamics to strategically upgrade or derogate particular peers in ways that increase their own social standing. In some studies, bullies have been shown to have superior perspective-taking skills and executive function abilities than other children. On the other hand, superior understanding can also be used to protect the self and avoid unfair victimization happening to you.

Finally, another interesting developmental change during the later years of school concerns children's growing sense of the *private aspects* of their own lives. Older children increasingly realize that matters of preference and choice, such as who their friends are, what music they like and what clothes they wear, are not matters of 'right' and 'wrong'. Hence they seek to establish greater control over such aspects of their personal domain as they get older. Gaining more control over such personal decisions appears to help to develop a sense of *autonomy* and *personal identity*. Of course, these are also issues that can lead to strong conflicts with parents or authority figures ('You can't go out dressed like that!'). Nevertheless, children and adolescents across cultures, including more traditional or collectivist cultures, defend their chosen personal domain issues with great vigour. This *cross-cultural similarity* suggests that defending one's personal domain is developmentally important for wider aspects of social-cognitive development. Examples include developing a sense of individuality, autonomy, and rights.

In parallel to the research on 'hot' and 'cold' EF skills, research into moral development has also focused on the unconscious role of emotions on moral judgements. It has been argued that people will *act first*, on the basis of their emotional response to a situation. They will then use reasoning to justify their actions. Developmentally, this post-hoc reasoning may be one mechanism whereby children gain deeper moral understanding. Research suggests that even young children consider issues of social convention (such as school uniform) to involve 'cool' affect on the part of those involved. They also consider issues of morality (such as intentional harm to another) to be 'hot' with emotional content. As moral and conventional reasoning become more nuanced, the important factors developmentally appear to be the same as the factors governing the development of reasoning abilities in general—working memory skills, executive function, meta-cognitive skills, and inhibitory control. Taken together, these are the main areas in which age-related changes are found in the later school years. Impairments in these areas will affect both cognitive and socio-moral development.

Chapter 7
Theories and neurobiology of development

Theories are explanatory systems for making a coherent story out of experimental data. Theories are useful for deepening our understanding of why children develop as they do. Theories are also useful for generating new predictions about child development that can be tested with experiments. Classically, theories of child development were based on *observations* of how children behaved at different ages. Two classic theories will be examined in this chapter, those of Piaget, who focused on the development of logical thinking, and Vygotsky, who focused on the influence of culture and language on child development.

Meanwhile, recent advances in neurobiology, particularly in genetics and brain imaging, are transforming classical child psychology. We have already seen examples in earlier chapters. For example, Piaget's proposal that 10-month-olds do not understand that hidden objects continue to exist has been questioned by EEG experiments with 3-month-olds (see Chapter 2). The EEG technique revealed different brain responses to *expected* versus *unexpected* disappearance, even though in both situations infants were looking at an empty location. Modern genetics is revealing the many biological influences on the *differences* between children. Although the environment will always exert an effect on child development, deeper understanding of gene-environment interactions is likely to impact classical developmental theories.

An example is the D4 receptor gene, which is linked to the development of inhibitory control. This gene moderates the effects of positive and negative parenting on children's self-regulation. Illustrative examples of recent work in neurobiology will be selected, and used to evaluate where the field of child development is likely to go in the 21st century.

Piaget's theory: the development of logical thinking

Piaget (1896–1980) was a biologist by training, and spent his first years as a researcher studying molluscs. He was very interested in how biological organisms adapt themselves to their environments. For the rest of his career, he applied this experimental approach to studying the origins of human knowledge. Beginning with ingenious observation of his own three children, Piaget developed a comprehensive theory of how logical thought emerged and changed with development. A key assumption was that infants were born with limited mental structures which were then adapted to the environment on the basis of experience. Each set of adaptations to the environment brought a partial *equilibrium*, but then new environmental features were observed which did not fit these structures. Hence knowledge evolved accordingly, continually adapting to features of objects and events until adult mental structures were achieved. Piaget proposed that children's knowledge structures passed through a series of stages which caused children to think and reason in particular ways at different ages.

The sensory-motor period: 0–2 years. Piaget's term for knowledge structures was *schemes*, and different stages of development were characterized by different schemes. During infancy and toddlerhood, thinking was limited to *sensory-motor* schemes. Schemes are organized patterns of behaviour for interacting with the environment. The baby was dependent on looking, listening, touching, and tasting to acquire knowledge, and on motor responses like grasping and sucking. These behaviours created rudimentary schemes, which then became co-ordinated, so that for example an object was grasped and then taken to the mouth. In this way, higher-order behaviour emerged from the gradual organization of simple reflexes, enabling *intentional* action. For example, an older baby might drop an object repeatedly in order to observe its trajectory.

Gradually the baby became able to *anticipate* the consequences of certain actions. For Piaget, this behaviour was evidence that the baby was beginning to *internalize* different sensory-motor schemes. The infant was conceived as actively *constructing* knowledge on the basis of interaction with the world. Piaget's theory that the child actively acquires knowledge has been very influential in education. This internalization of knowledge about actions and their consequences marked the beginning of conceptual thought: *cognitive representations*, independent of perception and action. Yet during the period 1970–2000, many psychology experiments were published showing that infants seemed to have cognitive representations for objects much earlier than Piaget had proposed. More recently, with the growth of 'embodiment' theories in adult cognitive psychology, the fundamental importance of sensory-motor knowledge is being recognized. Perceptual and motor knowledge are part of our conceptual knowledge, even in adulthood. So Piaget's focus on a 'logic of action' seems actually quite visionary.

The pre-operational period: 2–7 years. The mental structures that emerged from sensory-motor thought were described as 'pre-operational', as they were only capable of partial logic. A complete understanding of the logical concepts that govern the behaviour of objects and their logical relationships required further development. During the *pre-operational period*, children were busy using different symbolic forms (words, mental images) to change their action-based sensory-motor concepts into more highly organized mental structures. However, their efforts were impeded by various characteristics of pre-operational reasoning that prevented the development of a fully integrated system of mental structures. Chief among these characteristics were *egocentrism, centration,* and *reversibility.* Pre-operational children were *egocentric* in their thinking, perceiving, and interpreting of the world in terms of the self. They tended to *centre* their thinking on one aspect of a problem or situation, ignoring other aspects. Finally, they were poor at *reversing* mental steps (e.g., in a reasoning sequence) in order to arrive at a comprehensive understanding of a given problem.

The chief logical operations ('concrete operations') studied by Piaget were *conservation, transitivity, seriation,* and *class inclusion* (see Figure 8). The simple tasks that he invented to study these operations have now been repeated hundreds of times by child psychologists. For example, *conservation* refers to the understanding that objects like counters do not change in quantity when their perceptual arrangement is altered. Piaget argued that non-conserving responses were evidence for lack of understanding of the *principle of invariance,* that quantity is unchanging over perceptual transformations. The principle of invariance is a foundation of our number system and gives stability to the world of objects (see Chapter 5). Non-conserving responses arose because children might centre their attention on the *length* of the row of counters, neglecting other perceptual cues like 1:1 correspondence.

The pre-operational tendencies to egocentrism, centration, and lack of reversibility caused *disequilibrium* in children's internal mental structures. In addition, pragmatic aspects of conservation tasks, such as an apparently important adult altering one array and then repeating the same question about quantity, may suggest to younger children that they need to change their answer. If a 'Naughty Teddy' spreads out the row of counters instead, young children are less likely to change their answer. Indeed, more recent experimental work on the different concrete operations

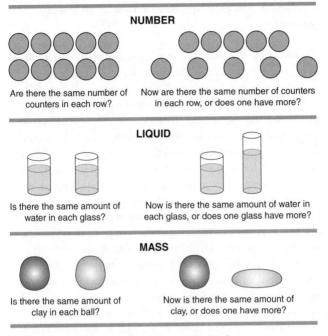

NUMBER

Are there the same number of counters in each row?

Now are there the same number of counters in each row, or does one have more?

LIQUID

Is there the same amount of water in each glass?

Now is there the same amount of water in each glass, or does one glass have more?

MASS

Is there the same amount of clay in each ball?

Now is there the same amount of clay, or does one have more?

8. **Some examples of Piagetian Conservation Tasks**

suggests that much non-logical responding depends on *aspects of task set-up*, both linguistic and non-linguistic.

More recent experiments suggest that logical abilities per se do not seem to be inferior in younger children. Rather, younger children lack the meta-cognitive and EF skills required to utilize logic effectively in various scenarios. Indeed, Piaget's theoretical observations about egocentrism, attentional focus (centring), and perspective-taking are really quite similar to current psychological notions about inhibitory control and attentional flexibility. Where the modern literature diverges from Piaget is in assuming a 'rich' interpretation of emergent logical skills. Rather than assuming that the logical structures required for successful reasoning are *absent* in young children, they are assumed present in a reduced form.

The concrete operations: 7–11 years. Pre-operational characteristics were eventually overcome when the child entered the *concrete operational* period. The concrete operations enabled abstract reasoning about concepts like quantity and number. For example, by applying the concrete operation of *transitivity*, a child could reason that $9 > 7 > 5$ without having to count out blocks to check the answer. Concrete operational thought was thus more flexible and abstract. Subsequent research has focused on showing that the concrete operations are present earlier than Piaget supposed. Yet a key issue is how 'competence' should be assessed. If a given concrete operation, such as conservation, is heavily dependent on linguistic and non-linguistic aspects of the assessment tasks, then how can we decide when conservation abilities are definitely present? This theoretical issue has important practical consequences for early years' education. Some educators believe that children should not be taught certain types of material until they are cognitively 'ready'. Yet teaching itself can push cognitive development forwards. Piaget's theory was more about the sequence in which knowledge develops, not about the particular *ages* at which different mental structures appear.

The formal operations: 11 years–adulthood. Piaget identified adult-like thought as the ability to *mentally combine* the different concrete operations. Piaget described this as 'second-order reasoning'. Adults and adolescents could mentally apply elementary relations like *transitivity* to objects and their relations. They could also combine (say) transitivity with 1:1 correspondence, forming new mental structures such as analogies. Piaget's formal operations were similar to propositional logic, a set of mathematical relations that governed hypothesis and deduction. Formal operational thought was thus *scientific* thought. Indeed, many of Piaget's tasks for exploring the development of formal operations involved hypothetico-deductive reasoning. One example is determining in advance whether a given object will float or sink if it is dropped into water.

Variability in performance in formal operational tasks seems to depend on the same factors as for the concrete operations. Younger children are usually hampered by lacking relevant knowledge, by having lower working memory capacity, by being weaker at inhibiting competing or irrelevant information, and by being poorer at reflecting on their own cognitive activities. Yet while a *mental transition* to formal operations in adolescence has not been supported, Piaget's focus on the 'logic of thought', with mental structures mirroring mathematical structures, could again be argued to be visionary. Most current advances in cognitive neuroscience depend on the development of sophisticated algorithms showing how knowledge structures can be created from the simple on–off responses of individual brain cells. This develops Piaget's view that cognitive structures should mirror mathematical structures.

Vygotsky's theory: the important roles of culture and language

Although Vygotsky (1896–1934) died young and did not generate a large body of experimental research, his ideas about children's cognitive development have been very influential. Vygotsky focused on the key roles of *social experiences* and *culture* in the development of the mind. While Piaget's focus was on the individual child generating her mind by herself, via action, Vygotsky argued that experiences *with other minds* shaped psychological development. These experiences included not only social interaction but also interactions with culturally produced artefacts for transmitting knowledge, such as signs and symbols (e.g., words, maps, counting systems, diagrams, works of art). The most important symbolic system was human language. In Vygotsky's theory, language was a *tool* that shaped cognitive development, guiding both thought and action. When young children merged speech and action, developing *inner speech*, language became the tool for organizing inner mental life. Indeed, as adults we intuitively feel that we 'think' using inner speech.

The importance of social context for cognitive development has been noted in previous chapters. For example, learning is optimal during episodes of joint attention (Chapter 2), and family discussions about psychological states provide an important context for socio-moral development (Chapter 4). Vygotsky was the first theorist to attempt to define *explicitly* how social, cultural, and historical forces shaped child development. His insights have had a particularly strong influence in educational psychology. Indeed, Vygotsky developed his theoretical ideas after being given responsibility for the education of 'pedagogically neglected' children (for example, children with learning difficulties). In his quest to develop teaching methods suited to all learners, Vygotsky articulated a number of important theoretical constructs relevant to psychological development. One was the concept of inner speech, which enabled the child to create a mental 'time field' of past activities and potential future actions. Another was the *zone of proximal development*, which was seen as critical for effective teaching.

The zone of proximal development (ZPD). Piaget had conceptualized children's thinking as unfolding according to its own timetable. Vygotsky emphasized the importance of *teachers* in extending the potential of the child. While (for example) an 8-year-old child might be capable of solving mathematical problems at an 8-year-old ability level when unaided, the same child might be capable of solving mathematical problems at a 10-year-old ability level when guided by a teacher. This difference between the developmental level for *individual* problem solving and the level of problem solving that the child was capable of with help was the zone of proximal development (ZPD). Rather than match teaching to a child's *current* developmental level, Vygotsky argued that it was crucial to match teaching to the ZPD. Children's innate potential should be discovered and 'taught to' for maximal educational benefit.

Vygotsky also recognized the crucial importance of play for child development. He argued that creating imaginary situations within which children could come to understand the adult world was a vital part of child psychology. As we saw in Chapter 4 with the fire engine game, during imaginary play children create and follow rules, the 'rules of the game'. Their strong desire to stick to these rules helps in the development of self-regulation (executive function) skills. Similarly, the *symbolic* functions of play, where a piece of wood can become a doll or a horse, enables the child to detach meaning from the real-world status of objects, and to operate purely in the imaginary (= symbolic) realm. Vygotsky argued that during play children were always operating in the realm of the ZPD. Thus in play, children were developing abstract thought. They were not being governed by perceptual and situational constraints. Vygotsky argued that teachers should capitalize on the importance of play by *deliberately* creating play situations for instruction. When a child learns something via active participation in play, then translation to individual understanding follows.

Vygotsky did not himself have the opportunity to test his theoretical ideas about children's psychological development with experiments. Nevertheless, the importance of learning via play, the importance of language development for further cognitive development, and the importance of the cultural and social contexts within which learning takes place, are themes recognizable in the research already discussed in earlier chapters. At the same time, some Russian psychologists have argued that Western psychology has misunderstood some of Vygotsky's key claims. For example, although Vygotsky emphasized the importance of the social context of learning, he also believed that teachers should *teach children directly* the knowledge that humanity has acquired over the course of socio-cultural evolution (such as mathematical knowledge). Vygotsky did not argue that each child had to discover this knowledge for themselves, via action and play. Rather, a symbol system like language could be used for direct transmission of such knowledge, via teaching.

Neuroconstructivism: a new theoretical model

As noted earlier, new insights from genetics and brain imaging are revealing various *biological constraints* on child development. Neuroconstructivism recognizes that biology will impact child development, and attempts to provide a systematic framework for understanding how this will occur. Severe genetic effects, such as hereditary deafness, are easy to recognize. In such cases, it is obvious that *accommodations* must be made to support child development (for example, teaching via sign language). However, most genes have small effects, many of which are not well-understood. These small effects nevertheless impact brain development and the development of the systems of brain cells (usually described by their location, for example 'auditory cortex' or 'frontal cortex') that underpin learning from the environment. Brain cells (neurons) exchange information via electrical signals. These low-voltage signals pass from neuron to neuron via special junctions called synapses.

Neuroconstructivism considers the action of *cellular changes* such as the release of neurotransmitters on psychological development (chemicals that affect how we think and feel by acting on the synapse). It considers the impact of *connections* within the brain, for example which brain systems interact directly (e.g., visual and auditory cortices, where the cell networks are only a few synapses apart) and which interact at a distance (e.g., visual sensory information acting on the attentional system, which requires neural transmission over more synaptic junctions). The broad framework of neuroconstructivism is shown in Box 1. It is clear that all the constraints shown in Box 1 will affect brain development and hence the development of mental representations (cognitive development). At the same time, very little research is available to provide examples of *how* each

Box 1 Biological constraints in neuroconstructivism

Constraint	Example
Genes	Gene expression is affected by the environment.
Encellment	The environment provided by other cells constrains neuronal development.
Enbrainment	The connections between brain regions constrain the functions of neurons.
Embodiment	The brain is inside the body, and the body exists in a particular physical and social environment which constrains development.
Ensocialment	The neural representations that develop are constrained by the social and physical environment.
Interactions between constraints	These constraints interact to shape the neural structures that underpin a child's development.

constraint affects child development. Therefore, rather than seek examples of how neural structures and neural networks are affected by constraints like *gene expression*, we will instead consider here what is known in general about the impacts of genetics and neuronal function on children's development.

Child development and genetics

One gene on its own can never determine the developmental trajectory of an individual child. Therefore, when considering the effects of genetics on children's development, it is important to emphasize that genes are *not deterministic*. The environment experienced by the infant and child will have a far bigger impact on psychological development than genes. At the same time, infants are not born all the same. Even siblings do not have exactly the same abilities and potential, even though they get their genes from the same parents. Innate aptitudes will differ. Some infants may become gifted musicians. Nevertheless, no matter how excellent the environment, not every child will make a great musician. On the other hand, we can certainly say that if a child receives no (or very poor) musical tuition, then that child is extremely *unlikely* to become a good musician.

The fact that genes influence development actually means that we should try and provide optimal early learning environments *for all children*, irrespective of their innate aptitudes. Individual differences will then emerge because of genetic differences. If some children experience very impoverished early learning environments, while others do not, individual differences between children will be much greater. Impairments in development due to a poor environment will be added to genetic differences. Revealing the genetic contribution to a particular skill or ability does not mean that nothing can be done to influence the *development* of that skill or ability.

Indeed, one interesting claim made by modern genetics is that many genes are 'generalists'. These genes have *general* effects on child development. The same genes can affect a large and diverse range of cognitive abilities. Very few genes act in isolation. While a single gene might determine something like eye colour, in practice most of us carry different variants of different genes that *together* make us more or less 'at risk' for a particular outcome (like becoming a gifted musician, or becoming dyslexic). At the same time, genetic inheritance acts alongside *character traits* such as motivation, and *environmental influences* such as quality of teaching and quality of nutrition. Further, quite specific environmental influences will apply to each of the cognitive abilities affected by the generalist genes. So if all of these trait-based and environmental influences are optimal, then the effects of the genes that carry risk will be minimized. So (for example), if a child who carries many of the risk variants for dyslexia is highly motivated to read, experiences an excellent early spoken language environment, and then receives excellent reading tuition from the first day of learning, that child may not develop significantly poorer reading skills than other children.

Example: DRD4—a gene for executive function? To illustrate the potential of genetic information in understanding child development, the example of a gene that helps to regulate the transmission of the neurotransmitter *dopamine* will be used. In general, when dopamine is released in the brain, we feel good. Dopamine is involved in reward and punishment. But dopamine is also involved in many other brain functions, for example cognitive flexibility. The dopamine D4 receptor gene, labelled DRD4 in the literature, has been studied in some detail because dopamine seems to be one of the primary neurotransmitters involved when someone deliberately focuses their attention. Therefore, when this neurotransmitter is not released effectively, it might be more difficult to focus attention—and to exert *executive control*.

We saw in Chapters 5 and 6 that executive functions are important for cognitive and socio-emotional development, and that individual differences in the development of EF skills are partly due to differences in parenting, language development, and working memory. Another source of individual differences in children's EF skills appears to be the DRD4 gene. In fact, one way in which this relationship works is that carrying a particular variant of the DRD4 gene called the 7-repeat allele seems to cause worse outcomes for children who experience poor parenting. The 7-repeat allele *decreases* dopaminergic signalling. This seems to disrupt the effects of reward and punishment on learning. For example, child carriers of the 7-repeat allele showed a stronger association between poor parenting at 10 months and anti-social behaviour at 39 months. 'Negative' parenting (see Chapter 4—excessively punitive, critical, and harsh) resulted in carriers of the 7-repeat allele showing higher levels of anti-social behaviour. In another study, children carrying the 7-repeat allele who had experienced poor parenting showed significantly lower self-regulation. A further study showed that positive parenting had a greater effect on the development of inhibitory control when the child did *not* carry the 7-repeat allele. This is evidence of a 'gene–environment interaction'. Carrying the 7-repeat allele interacts with the parenting environment in partially determining the development of EF skills in early childhood. So carrying this genetic variant creates developmental risk or vulnerability to developing poorer self-control in certain circumstances.

Other developmental impacts of DRD4. At the same time, it should be emphasized that the DRD4 gene has many other effects. One interesting one with respect to child development comes from a quite different area of development, the acquisition of reading. As the cognitive skills involved in reading development are relatively well-understood (see Chapter 5), many educators are developing computer software games to teach the component skills of reading. One Dutch study developed a computerized game for learning to read based on the most up-to-date research, and trialled it in a series of schools, selecting children who were struggling learners. Surprisingly, the game proved highly effective for some children, and not very effective for other children. One factor that determined who benefited from the game was the DRD4 gene. Children who carried the 7-repeat allele showed *reduced* learning of reading skills from the computer game. The reason seemed to be poor focusing of attention during the game, which reduced effective learning of the component skills.

This example highlights the 'generalist genes' perspective. It shows that genes will confer both positive and negative effects on child development, acting across many different domains. The actual influence of an individual gene will always be dependent on many other environmental and temperament-related factors. Nevertheless, a deeper understanding of how genes affect development will enable more individually targeted interventions. Presumably a different kind of intervention is needed to support reading for those struggling learners who carry the 7-repeat allele. As the genetic literature develops, individual targeting of environmental support for learning should become more and more refined.

Cognitive neuroscience and child development

Novel methods for creating images of the working brain have led to rapid increases in our understanding of the neurobiological mechanisms that underpin learning. Eventually, these insights seem likely to have transformational effects on the academic discipline of child psychology. For example, accurate information concerning *how* a child's brain actually develops a mental lexicon of word forms should shed light on theoretical controversies such as whether humans have an innate 'language acquisition device' (see Chapter 3).

Deeper understanding of the biological *mechanisms* of learning seems likely to be particularly important. For example, understanding the role of oscillatory neuronal processes in speech comprehension (the role played by the rhythmic on–off signalling of large networks of brain cells) may help to identify which 2-year-old children who are not yet speaking are at risk for a developmental language impairment (see Chapter 3). This is because we know from adult studies that natural fluctuations in brain rhythms (caused by cells sending electrical pulses and then recovering, hence fluctuating or oscillating continually from an 'on' state to an 'off' state) are one mechanism for encoding information. Natural oscillations in auditory cortex occur at some of the same temporal rates as loudness patterns in speech (e.g., as the jaw opens and shuts). To encode speech, the adult brain *re-aligns* these intrinsic neuronal fluctuations to match the same fluctuations in speech—so that the peaks and troughs in the electrical signalling approximately match the peaks and troughs in loudness as someone is speaking. Therefore, it is plausible that disruption in the *efficiency* of oscillatory processes may cause disruptions in language acquisition. Here I will just give two examples of questions in neurobiology that seem likely to be important for understanding child psychology.

1. *Do infant neural structures and mechanisms mirror adult neural structures and mechanisms?* One key question is whether the infant's brain has essentially the same structures (localized neural networks) as the adult brain, and whether these structures are carrying out essentially the same functions via the same mechanisms. If this were to be the case, then development would consist largely of enriching the connections between structures and (perhaps) developing novel pathways or functions via experience. This neural enrichment would depend on the quality of the learning environment.

The answer seems to be that the neural structures are essentially the same, and so are the neural mechanisms. For example, French researchers have used fMRI (which measures blood flow) to show that infants listening to speech while asleep activate the same brain areas that adults use for speech processing (left hemisphere structures such as 'Broca's area'). By direct recording of electrical signalling in the infant brain (electrophysiology, EEG, and magnetoencephalography, MEG), German researchers have shown that neuronal 'oscillatory alignment' to amplitude (loudness) modulations in sound signals, one of the mechanisms used by adults for speech processing, is present in 1-month-old and 3-month-old babies. The infant brain seems to use the same structures for processing language as the adult brain, and the same mechanisms. Other data for similarity in structure and function between adult and infant brains come from studies of face processing, mirror neurons, and working memory.

2. *Can cognitive neuroscience disentangle cause and effect in development?* A second question is how to disentangle the *causes* of development from the *effects* of development on brain structure and function. Most studies in developmental cognitive neuroscience are at present correlational. For example, a large number of studies with children of different ages show a significant association between the development of frontal cortex and the development of aspects of executive function such as inhibitory control. However, identifying which comes first (better inhibitory control, or more neural connections) has proved difficult. As with behavioural research, the key in going beyond correlations is to carry out *longitudinal studies*. The same children need to be followed for a long period of time, so that neural changes and cognitive developments can be understood in sequence.

An example of the kind of methodology needed comes from brain imaging studies of early literacy acquisition. The brain did not evolve for reading, and so as children learn to read, existing neural structures and functions are adapted to the task. Brain areas such as visual cortex (letter recognition), auditory cortex (spoken word recognition), cross-modal areas (linking print to sound), and motor areas (reading aloud) all develop interconnections that eventually comprise a neural system for reading. In one longitudinal study, 5-year-old English-speaking children were studied right at the beginning of letter-learning. When these children were first shown different alphabet letters, brain imaging (fMRI) revealed significant activation in visual cortex (the 'fusiform area'). This was unsurprising, as the children were *looking* at the letters. The children then experienced multisensory teaching about letters. They learned to recognize the letters in story books, to write the letters, to trace over the letter shapes with their fingers, and so on. Following this tuition, the children's brains were imaged a second time while they were looking at letters. This time, in addition to significant activation in visual cortex, the researchers found significant activation in *motor cortex* (the ventral premotor area). Hence although the children were not using their fingers or writing the letters, the *motor* (action) parts of the brain also responded to the *visual* letter forms. Studies such as this suggest that multisensory learning helps children in part because it causes multiple sensory recordings of the information—recordings which were not there prior to this direct teaching.

Looking to the future

Further neurobiological insights will clearly enrich our understanding of child psychology. Nevertheless, it is worth stressing that information from neuroscience will never *replace* the importance of understanding at the psychological level. The easiest and most effective way to affect a child's development is by providing the best possible learning environments in all aspects of the child's life—in the home and family, at nursery, at school, and in wider culture and society. So while knowledge that, for example, the development of frontal cortex is associated with the development of better self-regulation skills is important, the best way to *support the development* of frontal cortex is environmental. Children who are given opportunities for practising self-regulation, for example via spontaneous and guided pretend play, seem likely to develop a more adult-like frontal cortex faster than children who lack such opportunities. Cognitive neuroscience still has a major challenge in distinguishing cause from effect in child psychology. Given that the brain has around 86 billion neurons, it will take science a long time to figure out some of the challenges ahead.

References

Chapter 1: Babies and what they know

Ainsworth, M.D., Blehar, M., Waters, E., and Wall, S. (1978). *Patterns of Attachment: A Psychological Study of the Strange Situation.* Hillsdale, NJ: Lawrence Erlbaum.

Bowlby J. (1971). *Attachment and Loss.* London: Harmondsworth: Penguin Books.

Bremner, J.G., and Wachs, T.D. (2010). *Wiley-Blackwell Handbook of Infant Development*, 2nd edn Oxford: Wiley-Blackwell.

Gopnik, A.N., Meltzoff, A.M., and Kuhl, P.K. (1999). *The Scientist in the Crib: What Early Learning Tells us about the Mind.* New York: Harper Collins.

Rochat, P. (2009). *Others in Mind: Social Origins of Self-Consciousness.* Cambridge: Cambridge University Press.

Chapter 2: Learning about the outside world

Baillargeon, R. (1986). Representing the existence and location of hidden objects: Object permanence in 6- and 8-month-old infants. *Cognition*, 23, 21–41.

Fantz, R.L. (1961). The origin of form perception. *Scientific American*, 204, 66–72.

Spelke, E. (1994). Initial knowledge: Six suggestions. *Cognition*, 50, 431–45.

Wellman, H.M., and Gelman, S.A. (1992). Cognitive development: Foundational theories of core domains. *Annual Review of Psychology*, 43, 337–75.

Wynn, K. (1992). Addition and subtraction by human infants. *Nature*, 358, 749–50.

Chapter 3: Learning language

Clark, E.V. (2004). How language acquisition builds on cognitive development. *Trends in Cognitive Sciences*, 8, 472–8.

Eimas, P.D., Siqueland, E.R., Jusczyk, P., and Vigorito, J. (1971). Speech perception in infants. *Science*, 171, 303–6.

Fenson, L., Dale, P.S., Reznick, J.S., Bates, E., Thal, D., and Pethick, S. (1994). Variability in early communicative development. *Monographs of the Society for Research in Child Development*, 59, 5, Serial No. 242.

Fernald, A., and Mazzie, C. (1991). Prosody and focus in speech to infants and adults. *Developmental Psychology*, 27, 209–21.

Tomasello, M., and Bates, E. (2001). *Language Development: The Essential Readings*. Oxford: Blackwell.

Chapter 4: Friendships, families, pretend play, and the imagination

Baillargeon, R., Scott, R. M., He, Z., Sloane, S., Setoh, P., Jin, K., Wu, D., and Bian, L. (in press). Psychological and sociomoral reasoning in infancy. In P. Shaver and M. Mikulincer (eds-in-chief) and E. Borgida and J. Bargh (vol. eds), *APA Handbook of Personality and Social Psychology: Vol. 1. Attitudes and Social Cognition*. Washington, DC: APA.

Dodge, K.A. (2006). Translational science in action: Hostile attributional style and the development of aggressive behaviour problems. *Development and Psychopathology*, 18, 3, 791–814.

Dunham, Y., Baron A.S., and Carey, S. (2011). Consequences of minimal group affiliations in children. *Child Development*, 82, 3, 793–811.

Karpov, Y.V. (2005). *The Neo-Vygotskian Approach to Child Development*. New York: Cambridge University Press.

Leslie, A.M. (1987). Pretense and representation: The origins of 'theory of mind'. *Psychological Review*, 94, 412–26.

Chapter 5: Learning and remembering, reading and number

Carey, S. (1985). *Conceptual Change in Childhood*. Cambridge, MA: MIT Press.

Fivush, R., and Hudson, J. (1990). *Knowing and Remembering in Young Children*. New York: Cambridge University Press.

Gelman, R., and Gallistel, C.R. (1978). *The Child's Understanding of Number*. Cambridge, MA: Harvard University Press.

Goswami, U., and Bryant, P. (1990). *Phonological Skills and Learning to Read*. Hove: Lawrence Erlbaum Associates.

Nelson, K. (1986). *Event Knowledge: Structure and Function in Development*. Hillsdale, NJ: Erlbaum.

Read, C. (1986). *Children's Creative Spelling*. London: Routledge.

Chapter 6: The learning brain

Carlson, S.M. (2003). Executive function in context: Development, measurement, theory, and experience. *Monographs of the Society for Research in Child Development*, 68, 3, 274, 138–51.

Gathercole, S.E., and Alloway, T.P. (2007). *Understanding Working Memory: A Classroom Guide*. London: Harcourt Assessment.

Goswami, U. (2013). *Wiley-Blackwell Handbook of Childhood Cognitive Development*. Oxford: Wiley-Blackwell.

Hughes, C. (1998). Executive function in preschoolers: Links with theory of mind and verbal ability. *British Journal of Developmental Psychology*, 16, 233–53.

Luria, A. R. (1976). *Cognitive Development: Its Cultural and Social Foundations*. Cambridge, MA: Harvard University Press.

Chapter 7: Theories and neurobiology of development

Ashbury, K., and Plomin, R. (2013). *G is for Genes: The Impact of Genetics on Education*. West Sussex: Wiley-Blackwell.

McGarrigle, J., and Donaldson, M. (1975). Conservation accidents. *Cognition*, 3, 341–50.

Piaget, J. (1952). *The Child's Conception of Number*. London: Routledge and Kegan Paul.

Piaget, J. (1954). *The Construction of Reality in the Child*. New York: Basic Books.

Piaget, J., and Inhelder, B.A. (1956). *The Child's Conception of Space*. London: Routledge and Kegan Paul.

Vygotsky, L. (1978). *Mind in Society*. Cambridge, MA: Harvard University Press.

Further reading

Some of the experiments described in this book are discussed in greater detail in Goswami, U. (2008) *Cognitive Development: The Learning Brain*. Hove: Psychology Press. A fuller reference list is also available on the author's website at <http://www.cne.psychol.cam.ac.uk/>.

Other useful books include

Bloom, P. (2013). *Just Babies: The Origins of Good and Evil*. New York: Crown.

Donaldson, M. (1987). *Children's Minds*. London: Fontana Press.

Dunn, J. (2004). *Children's Friendships: The Beginnings of Intimacy*. Oxford: Wiley.

Fernyhough, C. (2008). *The Baby in the Mirror*. London: Granta Books.

Hughes, C. (2011). *Social Understanding and Social Lives: From Toddlerhood through to the Transition to School*. Hove: Psychology Press.

Lillard, A.S. (2008). *Montessori: The Science behind the Genius*. New York: Oxford University Press.

Schaffer, H.R. (1996). *Social Development: An Introduction*. Oxford: Blackwell.

Slater, A., & Bremner, J.G. (2011). *An Introduction to Developmental Psychology*. Oxford: Blackwell.

Slater, A.M., & Quinn, P.C. (2012). *Developmental Psychology: Revisiting the Classic Studies*. London: Sage.

Index

SOCIAL MEDIA
Very Short Introduction

Join our community
www.oup.com/vsi

- Join us online at the official Very Short Introductions **Facebook** page.
- Access the thoughts and musings of our authors with our online **blog**.
- Sign up for our monthly **e-newsletter** to receive information on all new titles publishing that month.
- Browse the full range of Very Short Introductions online.
- Read **extracts** from the Introductions for free.
- Visit our library of **Reading Guides**. These guides, written by our expert authors will help you to question again, why you think what you think.
- If you are a teacher or lecturer you can order inspection copies quickly and simply via our website.

ONLINE CATALOGUE
A Very Short Introduction

Our online catalogue is designed to make it easy to find your ideal Very Short Introduction. View the entire collection by subject area, watch author videos, read sample chapters, and download reading guides.

http://fds.oup.com/www.oup.co.uk/general/vsi/index.html